Number 344317: The Tale of the Forgotten Lion
© 2016 Diamond Cut International Press
A Diamond Cut International Press Book

Diamond Cut International Press, Permissions Dept.
2226 ½ NW 56th St. Apt. #1 Seattle, WA. 98107
Tel: 305-916-8693
www.diamondcutinternational.com
Email: diamondlife4all@gmail.com

Ordering Information
Please contact Diamond Cut International Press
Tel: 305-916-8693
Email: diamondlife4all@gmail.com

Author: Zackery Driver
Cover Design: Amelia Shroyer
Interior design: Zackery Driver

Manufactured in the United States of America
1st Edition, 1st Printing, July 2016

ISBN: 978-0692672426

This page is dedicated to my ancestors. All those who explicitly fought to make even writing this book possible and those whose mere existence was a revolutionary act in and of itself. It is also dedicated to those who are not yet seen, the seven generations to come after me...

Caution!

It should be noted that I began this book while incarcerated and possessing tremendous areas of unawareness. Now, however, I am on the constant journey of dismantling my own socialization, and my focus points have become Anti-oppression, Equity Building and Liberation. So, even though my current equity analysis includes recognition of gender, trans, racial, religious and the many underprivileged groups outside of the dominant culture, I have made the decision to keep my work in its original form. This serves my need for authenticity. It is also the purpose of my writing to show that progression and transformation are possible for all of us when given adequate space, support and education. I ask for pardon in advance, as being labeled a black male I acknowledge the privilege that this entails, as well as pain and discomfort that my decision to maintain the authenticity might cause anyone reading. On the other hand, being a black male has gifted me with an experience of oppression. That being said I stand in what I hope is allyship with you, knowing what it is like to experience my own perception of that sensation/feeling that cannot be named and knowing how it shows up in not only micro-aggressions but also in explicit violence based solely on our particular identity. In Solidarity, Struggle and Love.

P.E.A.C.E. To ALL my Siblings

"Nobody can give you
Freedom.
Nobody can give you
Equality or Justice
or anything.
If you're a man, you take
it."

Malcolm X

Dedication

This book is dedicated first and foremost to the sweetest and most beautiful woman in this world, my mother, the woman who brought me into this world and no matter what, where, or how I got there, rocked with me at the end of the day. She's been down since day one. You beat yourself up constantly and blame yourself for the predicaments I have found myself in but one thing I ask you to remember is that if it wasn't for where I came from, where YOU came from, where WE came from together, we wouldn't be where we stand today, nor would we be the people we are, standing in the position we are in, and today, we are great! Thanks for pushing me to write this work mama, I Love you.

To Astrid, an amazing woman who I have the privilege of calling my friend, confidant, and so much more. I don't think that you realize it yet, but you are a fucking FORCE to be reckoned with and have one of the most intriguing life stories I have ever heard. It surely has inspired me and pushed me to strive for even more in my own life. Thank you for all of the lessons you have already taught me and how to Love on a whole new level, you truly are an AMAZING woman.

To the object of my hopeless romance. I couldn't have written this work without the experiences we have shared together. You have pushed me to evolve and develop in ways that men twice my age have yet to comprehend. Our love and hate relationship has revealed so much of myself to me that I would have never otherwise realized. Thank you baby, I FUCKING love you, now and forever.

To Jacob Leonardi, the spitting image of myself in the intellectual minus all of the ego and bullshit! A man beyond your years, thank you young homie, you keep me on my toes! You are inspirational and I cannot wait to see where you are in 5 years from now. I have told you once and I will tell you again, the WORLD is literally YOURS FOR THE TAKING! DO NOT PROCRASTINATE ANY LONGER!

To those I have not mentioned but know that you have played a significant role in my life, especially those of you I had the opportunity to meet while incarcerated, whether it has been through just sending your positive energy and prayers to me or you have walked side by side with me on this journey we know as "life", know that I am forever in gratitude of you and the contributions you have made in the shaping of my mind, body, and spirit and its realization of who I am today, an infinite being and omnipotent child of the universe.

To every other sorry punk ass bitch who, living your life in fear, has tried to hold me back from the divine realization of self, who has casted negative prophecies upon me, who has tried to continue the division between me, my brothers and my sisters, and all of our innate powers and abilities FUCK YOU! And, this book is dedicated to you, too! If it wasn't for you, life would have been a walk through the daisies and I wouldn't be where I am at today. What would joy be if it wasn't for sorrow or ecstasy if it wasn't for weed? All jokes aside, I have broken through your traps and systems designed to enslave the mind and now I encourage others to do the same! As always, Death 2 My Haters is forever my prayer. I hope that one day soon you let your conditioned and disillusioned self die so you can wake up from the illusions you have been sleeping in and take back your freedom and rights as a human being as you exit the darkness and enter into this glorious light.

Last but not least to the streets, the tribal warriors therein, dope boys, pimps, hoes, bass heads, tricks, even the jack boys and to the penitentiary system as well, and all who are found within it from the booty bandit to the punk, the Imams and preachers to the gambling, lying, cheating, stealing hustlers, all the ol' heads, brothers endowed with wisdom to the young wild and reckless. I wouldn't be complete if it wasn't for you. You have been there for me every second of every day helping raise me when my father wouldn't and my mother couldn't, being there for me when I needed a friend or a foe when either was necessary for further development. Never having a problem with busting my ass! You bandaged the cuts and scrapes you gave me with pretty hoes, bomb Kush, ecstasy, and the ALMIGHTY DOLLAR!

Yes, your love felt SO good. If it wasn't for you, I wouldn't be as hungry as I am today. I wouldn't have the drive and determination that I do. Nor would I possess this unbreakable spirit found within me. Thank you, OH THANK YOU!!! My sweet beautiful forever tantalizing Concrete Mama!

FOREWORD

Π

What is a number?

Do they possess special powers?

Or are they merely the 1, 2, 3 counting of a child?

The quantity of how many toys she has?

As a teen numbers gained significance to me

Twenties, fifties, hundreds, and the Almighty Forty-Three

Engineers have used numbers to send spaceships to the moon

Our ancient ancestors too

Used numbers as something much more fundamental

Then the hated and dreaded simple mathematical

Equations or pages

On the bottom of your textbook

Numbers were metaphysical

Embodying the philosophical and the spiritual

Numbers were employed to give name to the divine

666

777

13

33

And otherwise

Other wise men have come in agreement

Numbers possess much more power then we at first glance see

Numbers from the dawn of time have affected us beyond what we currently conceive…

Why do you suppose possessing this knowledge they then numbered me…

344317

Introduction

Before diving further into the depths and crevices of my life story and psyche, I'd like to say to those who have only been in relationships with me while I have been exhibiting my intellectual or spiritual state of being there are undoubtedly going to be thoughts, words, actions, and stories herein that you would never in a million years associate with my character. But, for the sake of complete transparency and to create a work that reflects my life in its entirety and with the most pristine of visions, I have held no punches. I am serving you live and direct, uncut, raw, vulgar, and explicit excerpts of a true story, my story.

If while reading this you find yourself offended or in disbelief, remember that the stories in this book are the experiences I have endured in order to make me who I am today: the man that you may now say you love, admire, appreciate, or look up to. Alternatively, it may be that you currently hate or despise me for any unbeknown reason. Maybe you see through the goodness of my being into the "evil" inside of my soul. Whatever the case may be, first, be assured we all possess an "evilness" inside of us darker than the deepest abyss of the sea during an eerie late night. Secondly, my autobiography passionately testifies to how you will now most certainly have a reason to hate and despise me, because victoriously, I have overcome those very same barriers holding you down from enlightenment and liberation of mind and spirit.

(It should be noted that although I am being transparent with my own story, I have changed the names of certain individuals in this book to maintain their innocence and to help some save face. However, for those I am helping to save face, I must inform you that the mask can't stay on forever. You have to drink and eat one day and when you do you will be exposed… Or in the words of my mother: "What's done in the dark always comes to the light." Thank you Mama.)

1 = Knowledge

Knowledge is the root of all Understanding and Wisdom. It is the beginning of our awakening. The Fire and all spark of Self Realization. It is the corner stone of the Enlightened Being. Constantly and with diligence we must strive to seek Knowledge. And assuredly it is in all things.

Age: 23

"You have sixty seconds remaining." The automated voice said.

"Damn I hate that punk ass bitch, daddy! These phone calls are TOO short! I can't wait until we don't have to put up with this bullshit anymore!" The female voice on the other side of the phone exclaimed. Even with the blatant irritation she was expressing toward the phone call coming to an end, the woman had the sexiest, sweet sounding voice that you could ever imagine.

"Man, who you tellin' baby, don't worry it's not much longer 'til all of this is behind us and we move forward to bigger and better things." I reassured her.

She had been rocking with me for the last couple years of my prison sentence and had heard it all before. But, these words were the least I could say to try to bandage the feelings of loneliness she was experiencing without having the man she loved by her side, to hold her hand during the day, and to wrap her up at night as she dreamt of a better life. A life that she would never actually realize. At least not with me.

After a slight sigh she said, "Yeah daddy I know, it just seems like this is never going to end."

"You actin' like I don't know, I'm the one doing this fuckin' time. I only have a little longer though and this is the last time that I'll ever be back in this muh fucka. Believe THAT!" I could almost hear her eyes rolling in the back of her head, yet she didn't let her grief show through her words. I had to appreciate that about her. There was definitely a lot she could say 'bout the statement I made but she didn't. She chose to keep her conversation sweet.

"You sound irritated still. Are you going to call me back tonight?" She asked.

After only a few short months this woman had already begun to know me so well. We had never met in person but she could tell if something was wrong with me, if I was happy, pissed off, or holding something back just by the sound of my voice. When I thought about that it felt good that a woman, especially a woman as beautiful as herself, desired me and cared so much that she would take the time to learn me so well. On the streets, nah, of course that wouldn't be nothing to me, but at this time I had already been in prison for over two and a half years. In other words, to those living their life out there in the free world, Young Fresh was more like Old History. I was no longer a factor. I had become unimportant, but to her I was King. She saw through the bars and barbed wire fences. She saw me for the man that I AM and where I was heading rather than the statistic society had condemned me as before they threw me into a cage. Not to mention just talking for an hour with the phone service the prison had costed over $10! That meant for the hour in the morning and the hour in the evening she was spending $20 a day, just for the week, that bill is a minimum of $140. Now multiply that by 52!

"You have 30 seconds remaining." The unwelcome automated voice announced alerting us to the termination of our call in half a minute.

"Fuck--"

"Yeah I know baby I'm going to call you tomorrow morning a'ight. Aye, if you don't hear from me don't worry I have a lot of work I need to get done with my business plan, okay. I love you."

"I love you too baby. Have a good night and--"

The phone call ended abruptly and with that, the sweet escape of talking with a woman in the outside world was cut off. The reality of prison came flooding back into my mind. Particularly, the reality of the situation I currently found myself in. Automatically, I had to shift my mind into another gear. The soft sweet honey dripping that I was allowing myself to indulge in was over. Those tender words had to be replaced with vulgarity and the harshest language my tongue could muster.

Right now it was time to put the G back into gangsta and check this bitch ass nigga that thought he was hard.

While existing in prison, I saw things. I've seen guys who mistakenly thought that prison was a playground, that everything was okay and that they were safe and sound in here and nothing would ever happen to them. I saw guys talk shit and play games and go about as if things were not serious, as if prison was just another game in their comical life. I've seen the guys who listened to their parents' or girlfriends' advice: "just stay to yourself and do your time," "don't get into any trouble," "keep your nose in the books and don't make friends with people in there because they are not your friend and they don't care about you," blah blah blah...yea, that crowd. I've seen that for the most part, the guys who follow that advice are squares, lames, they quickly become the targets and marks of the ravenous behind these walls. They hop off the chain bus and fall right into sleeping their time away in a zombified state of mind thinking that everything is happy go lucky. Until, that entire illusion comes crashing down into a million little pieces in front of them, in one unfortunate moment-- when shit gets heavy and they're faced with violence and the explicit dangers found inside these iron cages.

On the other hand, you have another group of people who realize they have now just been dumped into a completely new culture when they entered into the prison system and it is in their best interest to hurry up and learn the ropes, rules, and regulations to this shit. They make alliances with other convicts because they realize that getting jumped in a thirty man shower stall with your asshole being left sore due to the fact that you had just become a victim of gang rape was not only possible, but probable. They foresee the rigid situations that are coming and prepare by making acquaintances, if not friends, with people around them through any common ground, whether it be the same drug of choice, color of flag, religious preference or race if nothing else or to some ABOVE ALL ELSE. At the end of the day you gon rock with those who you view are like yourself. Birds of a feather flock together type shit. Even in the second group of people you find those who are the greater and those who are the less, the weak and the strong, the predator and the prey, subgroups in the general grouping of people. To the strong, the hustler, and the predator the secrets of who's who, who's got work, what c.o.'s are loose, how to make weapons and other knowledge that had been learned through the years was imparted. Those were niggas who were with the shit. Down to push work, bust heads, really whatever's clever. These cats were with it. They were not hard to recognize especially if you're with the business yourself, game recognize game or in other words real recognize real. I put you up on this because unfortunately I wasn't born with a gold spoon *in my mouth, shit, not even a silver one, I am from the darkest, grimiest part of the streets and have been bred to be all the way with the bidness, cut throat. I ain't no big buff dude nor am I a bully I don't think I am the baddest muh fucka alive but when we talkin' bout this gangsta shit it's not ON me, it's rooted deep down INSIDE me, passed down through my blood. I know 'bout this shit because I myself was one of those imparted with the wisdom of these prison walls when I entered them. You could tell a lame that it was 'bout to go down, I mean a full out war and that he needed to sharpen up, otherwise he was going to DIE but that muh fucka wouldn't have the first clue of what the hell you were talking about nor would he know the tricks to that trade if you would. That was only ONE of the many things separating me from them, because for myself, sharpening up was something that I not only knew how to do, but I had been WAITING, just itching, for that opportunity to present itself so I could release some pain and anger I had built up inside.*

As I walked back to my tier I thought about the incident that had occurred earlier that day. I couldn't believe that this punk ass nigga really thought that even for a second I wouldn't check his ass and put him in his place faster than the jury found me guilty! Who the fuck did he think he was? More importantly, who the fuck did he think I was? Did he really think that I was about to let his infiltrating bitch ass test me and not retaliate? PUNK MUH FUCKA! When I was young I used to talk more shit than anyone and I did it with the best of them but ever since I got older I haven't been with the talking. If I got a problem you are DEFINITELY going to know about it, I ain't going to sneak diss you or play any games with it. First, depending on the situation I might let you know that I ain't feeling you or the shit that you doing but if it's serious enough to even warrant me saying something to you, chances are I'm going to come for your head. Case closed. That is why right now I have a pop bottle on my desk and I am breaking down this muh fuckin' pencil in my hands so that I can get the lead out of it to make this banger...

As I broke down the pencil sitting at my desk with my thoughts tuning out everyone and everything going on on my tier, I couldn't help but to go back to the basketball court in my mind and recall what happened earlier that day. *We were all hoopin' like we normally did, talking shit but having fun of course. However, today, after we had been going back and forth with the same two teams for the last couple days, the competition was turned up to the max. Everyone was playing their hardest and playing for that W, our pride on super swole and all of our hearts on our sleeves.*

After I had soaked one of my pencils in hot water, I was easily able to peel back the wood around the lead. With the lead out of the pencil, I broke the long piece of lead that was left into two pieces so that they could reach into the electrical socket in the bathroom;

then, I broke another little piece off to wrap up in a tissue paper that served as a makeshift spark plug. If you're lost right now, don't worry, it's okay; like I said, not even everyone in prison knew what was 'bout to happen with these tools, let alone the muh fucka who it was about to happen to. Let me give you a quick science lesson though; lead is a conduit of electricity, so if you ever come to prison remember that, it definitely comes in handy. Trust me. So back to Science 101: when I took the two lead pieces and stuck them into the electric socket, the electricity charged them up and they filled with electricity. Then, having that third little piece I told you I made, wrapped in the toilet paper, when you touch it to both the protruding lead pieces, it causes a spark that hits the toilet tissue and creates fire. BLING! It's perfect if you got a stick and you're trying to blow real quick in the cell and don't have the Afi, you're trying to burn some incense or whatever but for the purpose that I needed it for right now, it serves as something much more lethal.

With every second the game was heating up and becoming more intense. At first the other team jumped out ahead of us with a lead of five points, and that was a lot when we were only playing a game to 15. Everything was moving fast but my team was moving faster in trying to tie the game up. After the homie hit two 2's and I drove the rock in twice for two more points, we were now ahead by just one point. After their team got a quick pick on our side of the court, my man ran down the court trying to get a fast

20

break. But I was right there with him when he caught the ball as his teammate launched it down court to him. As he went up for a jumper, I ripped the ball right out of his hands, pushed back to my side, pulled up, and busted a 3, being that we were playing to 15 it only counted as two. Everyone in the gym started clowning my opponent; "Awwwww nigga you're weak!" "COOKIES!" "Why you let him rip you like that?!" Taunts and shit talk were all that you could hear. And just like any simpleton the nigga let everyone and their chanting from the sideline get into his head. When his team got back on their side of the court with the ball, my opponent caught an assist, and he drove hard with his shoulder down charging right into me. I didn't see it coming, and he knocked me right flat on my ass. Everyone called foul, but I flexed my chest and yelled "Nigga look at me! Do it look like I call fouls!? BALL UP BOY!" When the ball got passed back into play, I told our point guard to pass the rock and I turnt up. After crossing the nigga guarding me I got up in the air, freaked their center, and laid it up for another point making the count 13 to 10. All we needed was another two points and the game was over. They had the rock and they wasn't going down soft. A light-skinned nigga on their team drove right past the homie guarding him, hopped back and pulled the trigger for two, making the score 12 to 13. It was anyone's game but either team would be damned if they lost. I passed the ball into our point guard and as he turned around the fast-ass light skinned nigga, who just hit for two, ripped him and laid up an easy basket for another quick point tying up the score. This shit was too fuckin' close at 13 up. I yelled at my team to get their shit together; all we need is two! I called for everyone to post up outside and leave the key open to get the defense spread out just how I wanted them, then told our center to cut. While he did, our forward did too, making the D run into each other. I passed the ball to the homie as he was left open so that he could pull up. Out of nowhere the muh fucka who charged me batted his shit out of the sky! Not only that, but he snatched the ball back up and was running down the court. I tried to catch up to him, and just barely I did as he jumped to take his shot. I jumped with him, and as he went to release, I got my fingers on the very bottom of the ball just enough to change its direction. The ball fell short.

"Foul!" Phil the nigga I had been D'n up all game yelled. It was a pussy-ass call and everybody on that side of the gym knew it! It was bullshit! I didn't touch ANYTHING but the ball and this muh fucka knew that! He was reaching for any fucking excuse he could so that they could win the game.

"FUCK THAT SHIT NIGGA AIN'T NO FUCKIN' FOUL!" I roared back.

"FUCK YOU! YOU SLAPPED MY WHOLE FUCKIN HAND!"

"NIGGA ON THE MOB! FO' TRE I DIDN'T SLAP SHIT BUT THE FUCKIN BALL BOY!" I replied.

"NIGGA FUCK YOUR HOO--"

I jumped at the bitch ass nigga fast as I could before he could even spit out the rest of what he was trying *to say, hoping to tear his jaw off his face. Two of my homies got between me and the hoe ass nigga, holding me back from ripping him a 3rd new asshole! This bitch crossed the line dissin' my hood. There were a few things that you shouldn't do anywhere but especially in the joint, and that was to call another man a punk, a bitch, or disrespect his hood, and of course everyone hated a jailhouse thief. Break any of those and it was no more talkin' after that; it was straight to throwing them thangs! For me, it hurt even worse because for me, my hood was my everything. I wasn't from no simple street gang nor was I one of those dudes who just jumped on a bandwagon, my "hood" stood for my beliefs, everything I loved, and what I aspired to be, my dreams. I wasn't FROM Diamond Cut Familia, I WAS Diamond Cut Familia, M.O.B., I WAS 4Tre. I embodied Diamond Cut Gang and even had the initials tatted on my wedding ring finger to show my loyalty and allegiance. To add to the fire I was feeling all over my body, the muh fucka was now smiling as my dudes held me back, and that enraged me even more. My partnas were doing the logical thing, holding me back from fuckin' this dude up and possibly catching my 3rd strike but there was nothing more I wanted to do then to rip his head off of his fuckin' shoulders! "D, c'mon man you got an EFV on Monday man! This muh fucka ain't bout shit! You know that this mark ain't nobody, he's a punk homie and a snitch! Cut it out dawg it ain't worth it homie! CUT IT OUT!" They yelled but I couldn't hear anything they were saying. I could only see this bitch ass nigga smiling in my face. They got ahold of my body, and with the three of them now holding me, I couldn't get away from them. As I had learned earlier in my prison sentence, even though my body may be locked up, my mind can never be; and inside of it, I was plotting out some of the most diabolical shit that you could imagine happening to the human body with a prison made shank.*

I've heard it thrown around a lot that you should "Get down where you're mad at.", that's bullshit to any real Gangsta and sounds ignorant as fuck. Making a move in front of the police or in the eyes of rats isn't thuggin', it's mis-movin'. Real M.O.B. shit is calculated and plotted out, a chess move in cold blood not some Magilla Gorilla shit because your feelings are hurt and you're angry.

With my two long pieces of lead, the shorter piece of lead wrapped in tissue, a bucket full of paper, and an empty Root Beer bottle, I walked into the bathroom. After I set the bucket of paper down inside the sink, I placed the pop bottle on the counter and the spark lead next to it. I slowly inserted the longer lead pieces one by one into the electric socket right there on the wall inside of the bathroom. Once those were in place, I took the spark plug and touched it to the two lead pieces sticking out, causing it to spark up. The spark caught the tissue around the lead on fire, and I dropped it into the bucket. The paper quickly caught on fire. With the bucket's contents on fire, fast as I could I grabbed the pop bottle and let the fire inside of the bucket begin to melt the plastic of the bottle. As the plastic began melting, I started shaping the bottle into an arrow-head looking blade. The plastic was scorching hot and it burnt my hands as I formed my shank, but all I could think of was taking my revenge and gutting the bitch ass muh fucka who had dissed me earlier. As the bottle took the shape I desired for the blade, I worked the ass end of it, creating a handle swiftly; then, I dropped the shank in the toilet so that it would cool down rapidly freezing into the shape I had morphed it into. After it had hardened, I cleaned up the remains and flushed them down the toilet to destroy any evidence. Then, concealing my new best friend in my waistband, I walked back to my bunk. There, I had a roll of scotch tape waiting for me and I wrapped it around the handle of my banger til it grew fat to give me a handle to hold onto so that when I stabbed my enemy, repeatedly, I could do so without hurting my hand, or the shank slipping from my grip.

As I sat on my bunk, wrapping the last of the tape around the weapon I had just made, hot anger and the urgency I felt for going to reclaim my honor and respect consumed my body. I thought about everything that had brought me to this moment. I *thought about my life in prison and all of the losses I suffered while incarcerated. I thought about everything I had learned, everything I had gained, and all of my business plans I had worked so hard on and were waiting for me to accomplish. I thought about my mom and my baby sister, my ex-wife, the homies I made in and out of the joint; I thought about my younger brothers and all of my family and loved ones. I thought about the M.O.B. - 4Tre, the organization that I had created, believed in and stood for; about the first time I ever popped Thizz, seeing my mom getting beat while I was young and not doing anything about it, and I thought about my father who had neglected and abandoned me from an early age. I thought about the struggle of being raised by a single mother in poverty, her marrying a man that thought he could walk right into my life and claim to be my father. I thought about being sent to prison at the early age of fifteen, and all of the betrayals I had faced. It was my life that flashed in front of my eyes: not just the scenes, but the feelings and emotions that I had felt in the last 23 years and 8 months of my life and it flared my rage feeling all of that pain resurface. It fueled my wrath and propelled my actions...*

"All violence is the result of people tricking themselves into believing that their pain derives from other people and that consequently those people deserve to be punished."

-Marshall B. Rosenberg

2 = Wisdom

Wisdom comes in the Knowing and shines through our actions. Be Wise.

Age: Inception

23 years, eight months, one week, and exactly one day ago as I write this chapter, it was around 10:40pm on December 19th 1989. Outside, it was dark, but the night was clear, so the stars were visible and could be seen by anyone that happened to look up into the sky. We were in the month of the Sagittarius. The night was calm and quiet except for the chitter and chatter of those out on the town leaving the mall, restaurants, and shops; the transients, Salvation Army Santas, and officers of the law ensuring everyone's safety and tranquility. With Christmas quickly approaching, the holiday spirit could be felt in the air. You could hear the singing and humming of those who believed Christmas to be the most wonderful time of the year. The downtown streets of Portland were filled with Christmas shoppers taking care of their last minute holiday shopping. The picture was perfect.

Sitting atop a hill overlooking the metropolitan area however, inside Oregon Health & Science University was a different story. In room 187, a 19-year-old teen had been in labor for 13 hours. Right now, she was experiencing the most excruciating torment of the birthing process as her little baby boy's head began crowning. To some the scene would be horrific: blood, bodily fluids, and a child's head coming out of such a small and what usually is considered a lovely part of the female anatomy, now it was being WRECKED while the stretching and tearing of her vaginal walls allowed new life into this old world. To those who aren't so weak in the stomach however the event was majestic. The physical feat in and of itself was amazing, but the ethereal idea of someone somewhere going through the doors of death as yet another part of the infinite consciousness was approaching the tunnel of life in the shape of a beautiful new born baby, was baffling. This was the circle of life unfolding before the eyes of everyone present in the room.

My mom was there screaming to high heaven from the lowest depth of hell with the shrill voice of a banshee, for this little demon causing her so much pain to be taken out of her, yet, simultaneously, she felt a jubilant anxiety and anticipation. All this young mother wanted now was to look into her little baby's eyes and cuddle her first-born son. It had been a long nine months of cramps and pains. Not to mention the limitations that were put on this young woman's fast-paced life: the liability of harming the growing child inside her womb, the added weight gained while eating for two, and the constant stress of making sure to always protect the precious cargo carried inside of her. After all of the effort and hard work she had put in through the year, she definitely deserved the reward she was eagerly awaiting.

Unfortunately, that wasn't going to be the case.

As she pushed and pushed screaming with every contraction blood oozing from her Venus orifice intensifying the energy in the room, her baby, inch by inch, slowly crept from inside of her womb out into the world, bringing new life to the earth, or so everyone thought.

Push by painful push, it was happening; she finally felt relief as her child plunged through the birth canal accompanied by another little friend her bowels let loose (Fuck what yall are talkin' about, it's a normal occurrence; in fact, let's just say I was born THE SHIT!). With her endorphins running high, and the thought of finally being able to hold her baby in her arms, kiss him and look into his big brilliant eyes, all of her pain and embarrassment seemed to fade and give way to feelings of bliss. It was a euphoric feeling you only get to feel once with as much pleasure as you did your first time, like the first time you let heroin romance you as it travels through your veins, tingling your body and stroking your mind. Like the euphoria of the Black Lover, the joy my mother felt, however, was short-lived. In fact, in just a couple of moments, it would be completely destroyed. There was something missing in the room. The familiar crying and screaming of a newborn was absent, and there was only silence...

Hair sticking to her head as sweat and tears ran down her face, the proud smile of a new mother spread across her lips, her hands stretched to the midwife who helped in delivering me. My mother asked, "Can I hold my baby now?"

The midwife, Carol Howe, only looked at her with a blank stare in her eyes. My mother could tell that something wasn't right when the midwife only looked at her with eyes that were distant yet full of compassion and sadness, but she would have never guessed the news she was about to receive.

All the preparation and practice in the world would still not have made Carol ready to say what she inevitably had to say to my mother. With a deep breath, looking into my mother's young teenage eyes, with grief in her voice, Carol stated, "Sheila, I am sorry, but your son is not breathing. We are calling in a special team. Please be patient, everything is going to be okay."

She lied.

A muted state befell the entire room, while terror shook the foundation of my mother's very being. She franticly tried to put the pieces together in her young mind to understand what exactly was going on. Sitting straight up lightning fast in what seemed to be slow motion she watched as the Midwife turned to the right, holding me, a baby born dead, elevated in her hands and passed me to a group of scrub-clad individuals who would try their best to revive my eight-pound body and breathe life back into my tiny lungs. My mother was horrified by what was taking place in front of her eyes. It looked like a scene from a movie documenting the practices of the occult.

She couldn't take it anymore; she could no longer maintain her composure as the weight of everything was now sinking in on her, putting an unbearable amount of pressure on her chest. It was as if the room around her began to cave in on her while her world slowly spun away. As her hope and happiness imploded, her mind full of emotion and her body stressed to the max, she could do nothing else but erupt.

"NOOOOO! WHAT!? WAIT! WHAT!? WHERE ARE YOU TAKING MY BAAAABY!? YOU CAN'T TAKE MY BAABY!! PLEEEEASSSSE!!!"

The scream of a mother who has just been severed from her newborn pierces through the soul, enough to make the most hardened serial killer cringe as goose bumps take to his flesh; but imagine the sound of a lost and lonely girl, from a dysfunctional home of neglect and abandonment, who now finally had someone who would love her no matter her mistakes or how she looked-- it didn't matter if she had makeup on and her hair did or if she had on her tight jeans or just some old sweats, this baby was someone she could love that would always be there for her no matter what. But after nine months of anticipation as she carried me, I was being torn away from her in just seconds. She was left there with no family or friends to comfort her. She was all alone once again, and devastated beyond restoration.

Her baby was now gone...

It was as if the scrub-clad men and woman took me out of the labor room so that an angel could soar down upon me placing its heavenly lips upon my own issuing forth life through its holy kiss. Just as fast as the emergency team whisked me out of the room my infant lungs were blessed with the gift of breath and I was brought right back to be with my mother for the first time since the air of the outside world had caressed my flesh. There was and still is no explanation to why I was born unable to breathe or more intriguing how out of nowhere I gasped for my first taste of oxygen as soon as the team was out of eyesight but so it was. Was my life NEEDED upon this earth? My mother believed so. It was the first "miracle" I would experience in my life but by far not the last. As I grew up and the story was orated to me it was left for me to believe there was supernatural intervention that day.

As my mother held me, her little miracle baby in her arms she looked down at me smiling, her eyes beaming. She had her little bundle of joy, and to her I was the most beautiful baby boy that she had ever laid her eyes upon. She kissed me and held me so tenderly in her arms. All she wanted to do now was adore me, protect me, and give me the life that she never had, full of love, affection, positive attention, and support. The people in the room could literally feel the love from my mother oozing from her soul to her newborn child as she rocked me to and fro talking to me in a childlike voice and singing to me. When they asked her what are you going to name him? "Zackery Max Driver." Is what she answered. "Make sure you spell Zackery, Z.A.C.K.E.R.Y. His name is special." She declared with a sweet smile on her tired face. It was the beginning of an unbreakable relationship of unconditional love, forgiveness and affection. It was the birth of her first true love.

3 = Understanding

What is Knowledge without Understanding? As we progress in a society that KNOWS that this is a cell phone, this is internet and this is a car, things that we use every day, possibly are even dependent of, how does the Knowledge without Understanding separate us from our environment, natural law and order, other physical life forms and even ourselves... Can we fully Understand ourselves without the Understanding of the things we are co-dependent of? Things that are so much a part of us now that they are interchangeable to some for even their own body parts. I believe that if we asked, most people would choose access to cell phone and internet over holding onto childhood memories.

There seems to be a general disconnection between the Knowing and the Understood.

Age: Infancy-Four

A Letter from My Mother

To my dear son, my firstborn, Zackery Max Driver,

Let me first open up this letter with a disclaimer that my memory is not the best. Yet, I want to share with you some thoughts on the beginning of your life… Zack, your father and I wanted a baby. We tried for several months. You were conceived in Hollywood, California, just before we came back to Portland. I was late with my period so I went to Birthright to have a pregnancy test done. I do not know how to explain this all I can say is that the lady giving me my test said it was neither positive nor negative, to wait a few days and go back to the hospital and be rechecked. Anxious to know, I went to the hospital early. My test still didn't show positive or negative so they took my blood. It was then confirmed that I was pregnant with you. I was full of a variety of emotions, emotions ranging from excitement to fear. Fear due to being only 19 years old and not having my own place. Sadness because I wasn't married and I knew your father wouldn't be staying around or able to be a father to you. Excitement because finally I was going to have a baby; a baby who would be all mine, a baby that I could love unconditionally. I was excited that I was going to be a mommy. Your father was excited too. He wanted you to be named after him. I did not want you named after him. I wanted to name you ZACKERY. I chose this name as your father when I met him went by Mack and so I figured the closest thing he would get to being named after you would be to change the H to a K in the name ZacHary and I also wanted your name to have an E instead of an A as I wanted your name to be Zackery… Just like it sounds! Your middle name was after my father and I wanted you to have the same last name as me. So, your name was set in stone before I even saw your handsome lil face – Zackery Max Driver. I should have known from pregnancy that you would be stubborn. I had to be induced as you were two weeks overdue. I arrived at the hospital and was given medicine to start the child-birthing process. It didn't work. So, the doctor told me they would stop the medicine and the next morning if I didn't have you that they would start the process again. Well, the next morning came and there was not a baby born. They began inducing me again and this time they decided into the process to pop my water. Once my water was popped things started to progress. Here I was 19 years old and about to become the mother of a child. I was still a child. Yet, I felt I was ready and able to accomplish being a mama, your mama. Things started progressing on December 19th when I was told to start to push. I remember Trisha and Peggy being in the room with me and getting excited when they saw your hair. I was in disbelief that I was really going to be a mommy any minute. All I wanted to do was to hold you in my arms. To look into your beautiful eyes and to tell you that you will never have to worry that Mommy will be by your side until the day I die.

You were born at------. I had never given birth so I wasn't sure how things went with the birthing process. All I know is that after you were born and I didn't see you right away I was confused and scared. I asked where you were at as no one had you there by me. Trisha came to me and told me that you were having some problems that they were calling for a couple of the specialist teams to come. All I remember was that I was scared and then I began to pray... The moment finally arrived when I was able to hold you. I couldn't believe that THIS was MY baby boy. I couldn't believe that you were FINALLY here and I was looking into your eyes... You were PERFECT! You had all your fingers and toes. You were a handsome lil guy. You were so alert looking at me and I remember as tears rolled down my face saying to you that I will NEVER leave you and that I will ALWAYS love you. Trisha and Peggy later told me that you were not breathing when you were born and that that is why they had to call the specialist. The mid wife later came to check up on me and told me that I had postpartum hemorrhaging and that I was bleeding so bad that she was having a very hard time stopping me from bleeding. I was asked by the nurses if I wanted you to go to the nursery. My answer was a stern NO! After all of this I did NOT want you out of my SIGHT AGAIN!

As you started to grow and develop into a charming lil baby I was so proud of you. You seemed to always be way ahead of all the baby tests they do like first sat, crawled, etc. I could tell you were going to be a bright child. You brought me such joy. I loved being a mommy. I loved you with a love that I cannot explain… You were my EVERYTHING. Nothing was going to ever tear us apart! I remember one day going to check the mail and at the time you could walk slowly hanging onto my hand. On this day you spotted a cat and you fought and fought for me to let go of your hand. I kept telling you no. You didn't even care you kept struggling for me to let go of your hand. Finally, in frustration I said inside my head ok, you want me to let go I will. I thought for sure you were going to fall on your lil rump. WRONG! You took off with a couple of steps towards the cat! That was the start of you walking. Everywhere we went I was always being told that you were such a happy baby. I was such a proud mama. When I found out I was pregnant with your brother, I remember lying in bed with you telling you some names that I liked. When I said Joshua you got excited and said in your own little language "Joshua! Joshua!" so I knew I had to name your brother Joshua. You and your brother were two years, two months, and 10 days apart. You were excited to be a big brother and never seemed to be jealous. You always wanted to help me take care of him. I remember one day being at work and getting a call that the babysitter could not find your brother but that she could hear him crying. I started to panic, I told the babysitter to FIND JOSH! I was rushing to get out of work when the phone rang and my boss said it was the babysitter. I got on the phone to hear her say that you had put your brother in the toilet…

Thankfully, the toilet we had at the apartment was a VERY weird shape (one I have NEVER before seen nor to this day seen again.). You had tried to teach your brother to go potty and had dropped him in the toilet. Thankfully his head was not underwater. He was fine. I still left the office and came home to hold you both and to explain to you that Joshie can't go potty yet that he wasn't a big boy like you. I think you understood because you never tried again.

I remember Grandma Nancy had made you a Humpty Dumpty Halloween costume when you were almost three. I took you to Jantzen Beach to trick or treat and to be entered into their contest. You won First Place. I remember afterwards folks coming up and saying how cute you and your costume were. I remember too belonging to a teen mom group for a while and they thought you were SO adorable that they asked to have you on the cover of their magazine. You have always had such an adorable big, bright smile. Zack you have always been a bright child. You did good in school when you applied yourself. Another thing you were good at was trying to push the limits and breaking rules. I remember one time I don't know how old you were but perhaps three. We were outside talking to your Papa and we lived on a busier street. I had told you not to cross the grooves in the sidewalk and that you cannot be in the street. This day you kept trying to test me. You would go to the spot and I would tell you and you would come away, this went on several times. Then your little butt went right out in the street and stood there looking at me with a smile on your face and I ran to grab you…This was my second sign of you being a strong willed, mannish lil boy. You loved to be read to too. Books were your friend. Your favorite book was 10 Little Monkeys Jumping on The Bed. Your best friends during the first years of your life were Jacob, Caleb, your uncle Ron Ron and of course your baby brother Joshua. You LOVED music too. You LOVED to dance. It was so cute to watch you dance. I think you knew how to make your mama smile because you were always doing it and I was always smiling away. In fact I think you knew how to make EVERY woman smile, even as a little baby you were a flirt.

Life became a nightmare one day when we were driving down the street and you had told me that your fathers sister had abused you. I have to apologize. The first time you told me inside my head I was like no way, he doesn't mean that and thinking that maybe how you were saying it wasn't how I heard it. I didn't do anything that first time you said it... You then told me again and thank God this time I listened to you and in my head was like there is no way a child would say this unless it was true. I didn't want you to go through trial. I also wanted your aunty to get help. She was a teenager at the time and I knew that there was no way she would act like that unless something had happened to her. I just wanted to have a plea agreement so you both would get the help you needed. She plead guilty. You didn't have to go through a nasty trial. I was relieved for that yet scared to death how I could help you. I felt guilty and ashamed that I didn't protect you and keep you safe. I reached out for counseling for you that's when you met with a wonderful lady named Jan.

There have been many time when I look into your

beautiful brown eyes and try to stop the tears from coming out. I saw a lil boy who was violated in a way that I never would have imagined could ever happen to the little boy that I promised to be there for and protect. How could I not have kept you safe? How could I have not seen the signs of danger? How could I have not listened the first time you said something. The thoughts have flooded my mind many times in your life. I never wanted the cycle of abuse to be carried on with my babies. I was heartbroken. The abuse you went through is abuse NO person should ever have to experience. You did NOTHING wrong. You were an INNOCENT victim, a victim of sexual abuse, a victim of a system that did not protect you by holding her accountable to treatment. A victim to the school system instead of knowing and understanding that you were a little guy not understanding what violations you had experienced and why you were acting out in the ways you were to try to get the pain out... Instead of helping and supporting you they threw you into a prison they called a "School". This was the beginning of what I now know today of as you being in the "School to Prison Pipeline" and the beginning of a living nightmare for your life and mine watching my little baby boy walk through Hell.

4 = Culture/Freedom

When looking at Culture we have to agree that culture is created and sustained by Language. That being said just as much as Culture can create the space for Liberation which then in turn leads to Freedom, Culture, can also be oppressive leading to captivity and enslavement. The world as we know it is also known as the Universe, Uni-Verse, One Poem, One Song. Until the end of time Culture is tethered to Language. Not just the small sounds that leave our lips but the vibrations we call thoughts that are constantly in our minds. In order to change our Culture we must first change the language that we utilize.

Age: 4

It was over 21 years ago but I remember it like it was yesterday; actually I can relive the moment my innocence was stripped from the very essence of my being like it was happening right now. I have played it time and time again in my mind, consciously and unconsciously as I journeyed through my life. I can see my aunty vacuuming the floor as I sat on the couch watching cartoons on channel 42, the cartoon network. I can hear the vrrrrrr of the vacuum cleaner sucking dirt, crumbs and dog hair from the carpet. I can even see the episode of Dexter's laboratory playing as I sat there. A little child, clueless to the world, oblivious to what was about to occur in his own little world within the next few minutes, and how it would affect the entirety of his life... My life.

It was late in the evening. My mom worked graveyard shifts so she had me and my little brother babysat while she was away. This night, we were being watched by my aunty. I was sitting on the couch watching cartoons as she was vacuuming the living room floor. When she was done, I remember her asking me if I liked watching cartoons, and I said yes. she then told me if I wanted to keep watching cartoons, I had to go to my room and get undressed; and then I could come back out and watch them some more.

I went to my room, took my shirt off and came back out to the couch sitting down. My aunty looked at me and said "I told you if you want to keep watching cartoons, you have to take your clothes off." I told her I did take my clothes off, I took my shirt off. She responded with saying that I needed to take off all of my clothes. I refused, saying that it was cold; she insisted on bypassing the barriers I placed in her way. She prodded me again to go and take my clothes off, so I went back into my room and took my pants off too, and then came back to the living room to continue watching one of my favorite shows with just my underwear on.

I remember her sitting down beside me and putting her foot in my lap rubbing my privates with her foot. I hear her telling me to spread my legs; Spread my legs so she could massage my 4 year old penis with her

17 year old toes. Unfortunately, this wasn't enough for my aunty; she wanted more, she needed more. She told me to follow her to my mother's room where she got naked and laid back on the bed. She told me to take my underwear off and to get on top of her, and then guided my body in between her thighs. I don't remember sensing any sensations; I don't even know if my four-year-old penis could get hard; even if it did, how it would penetrate a nearly grown woman. Being able to look back with a little more knowledge, I realize what I was experiencing was a numbness brought on by the psychological shock and trauma I was dealing with in the moment. After she had coached me through grinding my hips against hers and kissing her breast, she informed me she was done with me and to get dressed and go to bed. I felt so confused. I remember while she was raping me, she kept saying she loved me and asking me if I liked it as she caressed my body; so when she went cold, I felt discarded, neglected and abandoned. I was empty.

At 4 years old, I didn't know how to cope with what I was feeling by myself. I felt like I needed to talk to someone about it, so I told my mother. I didn't know then what she thought when I told her "aunty touched me mommy." But the coldest part about it is that my mother just acted as if I was trippin' or playing some type of game. when I reached out to the only human being that I was close to, who I thought had my back and would protect me from the strange things occurring in the world, she shushed me and made me feel like I was worthless, without a voice, and didn't matter, by not listening to me or seeing the confusion and pain that was stirring around in my young mind, punishing my soul.

It wasn't until the second time that I brought it back up to her that she put any weight in the words that I was saying to her. She eventually heard my cry for help and listened to me. That is when she took action and brought it up in the court, and found a therapist to work with me through the experiences I had underwent with my aunt. It was the beginning of even more problems for me in this life however, because after her bringing the law into our family my father's side of my family, from which my aunty who had molested me was from were extremely angry with my mother for snitchin on their sister and out of their anger stopped communicating with not only her but me as well. When I opened up my mouth for help in getting through the confusion and hurt that I was experiencing inevitably I lost half of my family that day. In fact I would go as far to say I lost half of myself. They were the only black people that I was around at that time in my life. a time where a child is going through the developmental processes and starting to craft their ego, who they were and how they would show up in the world and now my identity was missing half of itself with my family missing and my culture only being taught to me through music videos, my mother's boyfriends and want to be gangstas that I would see for a moment or two on my way to school or around my neighborhood.

There were two things that shifted my psychology outside of how my perspective towards sex began to be molded throughout this experience in my life. 1, due to the ignorance I would unfortunately face around my own culture I grew to be fearful and intimidated by my own people being that the only image I had to stand on for myself and then project on others was a heartless gun toting ready to kill individual only knowing violence and crime and the only accepted emotions being that of anger and rage. The 2nd thing was that when my mother had found me a psychiatrist she had linked me to an older woman to do therapy with. This was the first woman in my life that I felt heard or seen by, the only woman I ever experienced who listened and back then not knowing the way of the world thought was genuinely concerned with me and my well-being not just doing her job. How I see this showing up in my life today is that I am 7/10 times finding myself dating woman that are older than me by at least 5 years but even upwards of 25 years older in some cases. people have asked me before why is it that I am attracted to older woman and I have told them that I do not know or told them well older woman have more experience so they are better in bed however after dissecting my time with Jan, I realize that I do know, and that it is much deeper than an older woman knowing how to please me sexually. I see now that I was conditioned even then, to look for the only woman who showed me her undivided attention every time I was with her and relive those moments in my adult life now by seeking the company of women who are older than me and can provide that selfless maternal nurturance

I have always craved yet lacked. A nurturance that although my mother "loved" me to death was unable to give to me herself because she was actually loving me TO DEATH, NEEDING me and NEEDING my Love instead of freely giving me hers. She was codependent of me and it showed by how she swamped me with her affection and attention. The difference at first between a parent who loves their child versus one who needs their child on the outside may not look very different but especially as children we are able to pick up on the most subtle of things from body language all the way down to the energy and vibration of emotions and intent. This is because when we are young we are most intuitive, closer to the spirit and not yet conditioned by society. I felt a vampiric need of my love and validation from my mother, although at the time I could not come anywhere near articulating it I could feel my energy being absorbed by her when she held me, when she told me I love you anticipating and expecting me to say it back, when she demanded that I gave her a kiss good night or that if I didn't have anything nice to say not to say anything at all. These without her knowledge were all factors that led to me abandoning my True and genuine Self and picking up the role of the people pleaser amongst other mask and the violence I was inflicting on myself. It became ingrained into me at this early age that I HAD to smile, I HAD to be generously kind and artificially polite which only pulled me further and further away from the authenticity of who I am but filled her cup. She was in need of something to meet her need to matter and she found it in me. Unfortunately, there were no boundaries around her needs and my needs as a child so it warped my ideology of what a relationship would look and feel like when I was ready to date and it also left me needing the partner that TAKE care of me vs. care for me and meet my needs for me, the needs that were not met when I was a child.

It would be great if the tales of misery ended there with being sexually abused by a family member however there was so much more instore for me that no one could have guessed was going to occur the way it did. I guess in order for me to Truly appreciate the feelings of happiness and joy the universe saw it fit that I experienced their polar opposites such as betrayal, abandonment, depression and turning my anger inwards to the point where I began to hate even myself. Seems this had to happen before I could be blessed with experiencing my higher self and living consciously.

Life was constantly crazy then. The chaotic dysfunction began to become the norm. I was six years old when my mother had introduced me to one of her boyfriends for the first time. He moved in with us shortly after that and when he got comfortable living with us I was also introduced to domestic violence. I remember being so scared at first, like heart pounding, frozen, don't forget to breathe scared the first time I heard his super aggressive yelling and walked in only to see my mom trying to cover her face to protect herself and a full grown man reaching as far back as he could to rain down punches on top of her. Looking back I feel so ashamed and defeated because I can remember telling him to stop hitting my mother and then that anger and aggression being turned towards me and it scaring me into submission. I was so scared I allowed my mother to continue to be beat on mentally, physically and emotionally, to be spiritually destroyed right in front of my face. I can clearly imagine driving to my grandma's house and hearing the impact of a fist against skin when for no reason my mom's boyfriend punched her in the eye while she was driving down the freeway and when she pulled over another barrage of hard punches landing on her soft face as she was ordered to continue driving… I remember being paralyzed in fear observing all of this. My honor and respect for my mother being sucked out of me when I heard her lie on behalf of her assailant when my grandma asked her why her face was all bruised and she answered some photo albums fell on her while she was moving things in the closet. I watched my mother take being slapped, choked, yelled at, pinched, bit and verbally abused for what felt like every day just to take it and accept it. It saddens me that I have to admit this but instead of standing up for her I began to see her as dirt myself and empathy for my mother was replaced with anger, shame and embarrassment. This was so true between her obesity and the way she allowed herself to be mistreated that one day when she was picking me up from day care right in front of her when asked if she was my mother I looked at her embarrassed and disgusted and told the boy asking me "No that's not my mom. She is my baby sitter"…. Those words haunt me to this day… The more insight I gain and time I spend looking at the circumstances that led up to every event in my Life I begin to Understand and have empathy for myself though because I see the ways in which I was being conditioned to respond exactly how I had. (This is why it is of the utmost importance to not only guard your brain, no you CANNOT stop there! YOU MUST also run towards the positive things, run towards the conflicts which will create growth, you must run towards coming undone and removing the rocks in your path with determination and commitment and subscribe only to excellency and creating the best version of yourself because then you will also become the manifestation of THAT conditioning and that conditioning leads to Greatness. All this while understanding and forgiving yourself when you fall short of how you would like to be or act in the world).

One of the worst experiences she had to endure happened right in front me but fortunately it was the catalyst to her taking her life back into her hands and getting out of the cycle of domestic violence. I remember it being Sunday morning, we were the family that went to church every Sunday... So, as I was saying, we were getting ready for church which meant that we were preparing our Sunday finest, Devon my mom's boyfriend was ironing all of the clothes and my mom said something he didn't like and just like that he lost it and began to yell and scream at her. it seems like it happened in slow motion but fast at the same time as he lurched forwards at her and with one hand began choking her and with the other pressed the hot iron into her flesh, I can hear the sizzling of her skin under the irons searing hot temperature, I could see the smoke rising from her burnt skin and smell her flesh burning under its heat, I saw the pain shoot from her body into her face and all of the misery and feelings of powerlessness and hopelessness rise into her face as he abused her. As he pressed that fucking iron harder against my mother and yelled at her "You want to talk crazy bitch, you got me fucked up you fat bitch, shut your fucking mouth, you better not say shit or I'm going to kill your punk ass"

For the rest of my life I have to live with the burden of not only watching these hardships happen to my mother but also knowing I did so without even trying to protect my mother and worse because this excuse for a man was my only father figure, he was a gang-member and he was black I had begun to look up to him and start looking down at my mother to the point that when he had put his hands on my mom I too began to yell at her and tell her quit crying as in my little mind I was beginning to feel she deserved it or maybe it was that her taking victim stance gave an outlet to the pain and hurt I was feeling already inside and through this I could vent. Even with 20 years passed as I write this I still feel shame, embarrassment and worthless for my cruelness to her in those tragic times of her life. I often fantasize about being the 6' 200 lbs. full grown man that I am today and being placed back in those situations and, OH, how the tides would turn! Oh, how great it would feel to snatch Devon by the back of his neck and see the same horror on his face that his actions put upon my mother's! Then with all the vengeance in the world smash his face into concrete and gravel. Continuously smashing it until there was just a tangled mess of blood, cartilage, bone and exposed flesh where his face used to be... Oh how I wish I could kill him. How I could torture him and take out all of the pain I have experienced on not just his body but his soul. If I could use the iron on his skin, if I could violate him, if I could make him experience the same fear and deep anguish and pain that I experienced... AAAAARRRRRRRRRRGGGH!

It was with all this chaos brewing inside of me, with all these feelings of anger at Devon and my mother, hurt and pain from the betrayal of my family and the loss of my father himself not because he died in valor but because he chose to neglect and abandon me and my brother to chase the fast life, it was with feeling inadequate, with feeling hopeless and powerless over even my own self, and with the negative self-talk of "I am not worthy" playing on repeat in the back of my head that I entered into the world, grade school specifically and as I am sure you could imagine getting through these tragedies did create strength and such a tolerance and patience that I would undoubtedly need to survive on the journey that was to come ahead however, it didn't make for the picture perfect beginning of my life... whatever that is supposed to look like. In fact it pressed my spirit so far deeply down inside of me that even if I wanted to I wasn't able to be me, Zackery Max Driver. I was so ashamed, so oppressed, so timid and easily influenced that I began to take on the personality of whoever I was with or the group, I tried to fit in and be who I thought they wanted me to be and continued the cycle of alienation losing my uniqueness until I had had too much and everything that was stored and locked up inside of me was bubbling up, all this rage, all this anger, all this pain was just ping ponging inside of my belly, my chest, my neck and my head. It had come to a head, it had to come out, without the words to articulate it I felt if I held this in any longer that I was going to explode and…

Age: 6…

"Fuck you bitch! I'll kill you!" That was my war cry as I launched a chair at my teacher, the woman who took up the responsibility to educate my young mind. I was in the middle of a rage that was created by the feelings of inadequacy, depression, hurt and self-destructive anger, due to my needs to be seen and heard not being met. But wait, don't those words sound vaguely familiar… "Fuck you bitch, I will kill you"…? Yes, they were the exact same hate filled words I was hearing my mother's boyfriend rain down upon my mother in my home. At 6 years old and living in the dysfunctional environment that I was part of. I had absolutely no coping skills to deal with the internal pain and conflict I was facing on a day to day basis and my only healthy outlet which would be Jan (my therapist) was already off limits and blocked because my mother and her boyfriend had already conditioned me to believe talking about family problems such as watching your mother get her ass beat on a daily basis, was not to be spoken about not only outside the 4 walls of our household, but even inside as well. This mental prison was fortified with statements such as "If you say anything to anyone

CPS will take you from us" or "If you say anything the police will come and take your dad to prison"

It was the beginning of internalizing my problems with no relief, directing my anger in words instead of expressing it externally and dealing with it productively. It was the beginning of a road of sabotage and destruction, of lacking empathy, hating myself and not trusting others. A life void of ANY confidence and all the feelings of unworthiness compiled upon me till I had no self-esteem or belief in myself. This was what led me to throwing my chair at my teacher, the woman putting her time into building me up. These conditions are what lead me to chasing my teacher around her desk with my pencil threatening to stab her. These are the circumstances I was waking up with every morning that led me to blurting out random vulgar comments in class, yelling at my teachers and making sexual comments to the other students in my class. I wasn't empowered to be honest and transparent about what was going on for me in fact I was explicitly told not to, therefore, I had no system of working with my problems and getting my needs met, so the only option left... I acted out the dysfunction I was caught in. I pushed or yelled to be seen, I acted out to be heard, I acted out to receive the attention and to feel any type of connection and care from people around me who had no idea what HELL I was going through at home, and the level of disconnect and alienation my existence existed in. It wasn't because of a lack of skill or academic talent but it was for THIS undealt with pain and trauma why I was pushed into a behavior modified classroom in the first place or alternative classroom as some know it, schools and classrooms where teachers knew more about physically restraining children than educating them. Schools where there was a team of staff WAITING for a child to misbehave instead of encouraging them to achieve good grades. A school where the doors locked behind you and this is why before it was popular in the Bay area to "ride the little yellow bus and go dummy retarded" I was riding the little yellow bus feeling all of the embarrassment I could stomach when I went to and from my place of "education".

Looking back when I was young I realize that I had no true sense of vision. I couldn't see my future therefore I had no care for it. The phrase "Out of sight out of mind" resonates here. Yes, there were people telling me that education was necessary and I knew intellectually that it wasn't the best idea to act up in class but I had no concrete vision, I had no relatable role model or experience that said you get these things when you apply yourself in school and this is one of the steps to wealth and success that it was mandatory to not only go to school but to really dedicate and commit to it and get good grades. It was all hearsay because everywhere I looked around me I saw poverty, there were no indicators of ease or success based off of education. And furthermore, I didn't realize that the consequence for talking back to my teacher, fighting with other students, making snide remarks would result in me receiving a subpar education, which would result in a lack of career choices, which would further result to perpetuating the cycle of poverty I was stuck in and the mind state that resources were scarce. This then would lead to the desperate feelings that one feels right before he decides to commit a crime resulting in incarceration, that is, if you even make it that far before you get incarcerated in the first place, or killed. And I even take that back, let's be honest, in the classrooms I had access to, that I was PLACED in, there was no "education". The word education actually has several roots two of which are the Latin 'Educo' meaning to DRAW OUT as well as 'Educare' which means TO REAR OR BRING UP... In these classrooms especially and even in the public school system at large there is no DRAWING OUT, instead, we were told to memorize instead of to think critically, to just accept instead of asking questions and finding out, searching for the truth, we'd memorize and then be asked to regurgitate colonized tradition and fabricated history.

There was OPPRESSION and SUPPRESSION of our youth and the raw energy we exuded. There was no REARING or BRINGING UP, there was "SHUSHING", there was FULL-NELSON RESTRAINTS and 250 LBS MEN SITTING ON THE NECK, BACK AND LEGS of us lost wild youth trying to find our place. Trying to find the Love and attention, the affection our mothers' weren't giving us and the strength and roots our missing fathers were unable to provide. We were the discarded children of the public school system and society at large who really only showed favor to those possessing 2 parents, a house with picket fence, a dog and salary way above the 40k poverty line all of our families were well below being the targets of oppression and exploitation. But this was Life and this is where I was crafted, in the womb of the beast. It gifted me the skin of a dragon, the roar of a Lion, the keen sight of an eagle, the humility of a turtle, the flexibility of a chameleon and the wisdom of the great old owl. It was my stage prep, the teaching I would need to endure the trials and struggles of the tribulations to come and yet somehow through all of the violence, through all of the chaos and through all of the pain I was able to hold on to my Self, a sweet spirit, a Loving spirit, or maybe it was the other way around. Possibly from going through all of the havoc and pain it softened me, possibly it cracked this socially constructed reality I was born into and gave invitation to the light, maybe it bore a hole deep enough inside of me to hold the capacity to Love. Or a less attractive idea, maybe it made me NEED to Love and be loved by others... To need to be seen by others more than I needed to see myself.

Not only did I need Love I needed to be accepted, I wanted to be cool, I wanted to fit in, I wanted to be part of something bigger than myself! It was in the midst of all these desires for love and connection that the sound of my own voice was lost. My desires to be the cool guy and to have nice clothes in hopes of creating self-worth, feeling better about myself and getting the attention of other people were stronger than my desire to just be me. Because I was afraid to be me meant that I would be lonely, that I wouldn't be cool and that I wouldn't have real friends. Because even with the people that were drawn to this image I created of myself there was no authenticity there so the real me under this mask was always lonely and the relationships never lasted long because who I presented was different then who I was, there was no point in which we could connect at and as that was figured out I was discarded again. Because of the socialization and conditioning I experienced I thought to be me, the loving, caring, gentle and supportive person I was inside behind all of the walls I put up meant I was being a bitch or a punk or not a real man. With all of the messages coming in from the music I was listening to, the guys in the street who had a nice car and beautiful woman around them, the movies even the video games I played they all sent me a message that said to be a black man meant to be a drug dealer, to be a black man meant to be a pimp, to be a black man meant you had to kill someone over your tennis shoes, and I wasn't even human, I was a sexual fetish of white woman and plain out sexualized period. I began to set standards for how I would conduct myself that were contradictory to who I truly was on the inside only to make myself feel even worse than I already had about me. In the midst of these complexities is when I met Matt. He was from around my neighborhood, an OG blood who happened to now be selling crack… and one of his best clients? My mom's undercover crackhead boyfriend Devon. Yea, imagine that. and I am still mad at that little bastard not only did he beat on my mom as if that wasn't enough but this muh fucka had the audacity to steal my got damn Nintendo 64 video

games and sell them so he could get high…
FUCKING BASTARD!

Matt one day while I was at his place started counting money and being as young as I was it was a LOT of money. I asked him how he got all that money and the rest was history. He showed me a little white chunk of something that was hard, kind of oily and smelled odd, he told me that it was "work" (Slang term for Crack Cocaine) and it was worth $10. He instructed me that "all you have to do is give somebody 1 of these for every $10 dollars they give you, and if they give you $25 give them 3."

My first day was amazing! Instead of having to go to school for the possibility that I might get paid 15-20 years down the road I sat in a house all day playing video games and when one of the smokers knocked on the door and handed me some money I quickly counted it and then gave them their money's worth and was paid right then and there. Looking back I surely was a fool because I was given only $100 out of what was probably well over $2k but I was young and HEY! A cool grown up was saying I was a gangsta and his little homie. It made me feel GREAT! For the first time in I don't know how long, I was proud of myself, I felt on top of the world, and unfortunately this was just reinforcing the messages I was receiving via mainstream media.

5 = Power/Refinement

Hahaaa, I remember the first time I smoked weed, no, let me rephrase that, I mean yeah I remembered the first time I "smoked" too but what I'm laughing at is the memory of my young ass the first time I got high! I mean REALLY got HIGH! Ha-ha, yea don't front! I know I wasn't the only one calling out for Gods help and safety in my time of weed, whoops, I mean need, I was swearing up and down that first time I got high that If Jesus would let me live I'd NEVER smoke again, but despite my prayers the world kept spinning no matter how hard I prayed. Shit, I must have been a freshman, and yeah, of course like most I wanted to hang out with the older kids and try to prove I too was cool and with the shit (shaking my head now as I am 26 and writing that… Oh the folly of our youth) I think it was lunch break, we left Franklin High School the school I was seldom attending and hit some cuts to an apartment where apparently some old white guy didn't mind us smoking as long as he got a little action out of the deal as well. (Seems just a tad bit creepy if you'd ask me now, But hey, he let us smoke there so let's give him the benefit of the doubt and say he was just a hippie ahead of his time in 2003… ahh man, Fuck I'm getting old). So, I remember it was me and a couple of the homies from school, 7 Dice, Baby U and another cat I am not even going to mention in my book because he was a foul character and as I said before I won't be exposing people just my own story and Life. I remember "hitting" the weed, just sucking the smoke into my mouth like the other couple times I had "smoked" … "Ay man! Fuck nah, you ain't about to waste THIS weed, you haven't ever smoked before boy, have you!? Nigga hit that shit for real! Fill your lungs up and hold it in!"... Trying to be cool and fit in, you KNOW what I did next... ------------ COUGH COUGH COUGH! Everyone in the room erupted laughing at me as I coughed and struggled to breathe, they thought this shit was funny, I thought I was about to die! It seemed as if just when I got my coughing back under control the blunt was being handed to me once AGAIN! "Nah, I'm good" I said. It seemed as if all in unison my FRIENDS quickly shouted in response "Nah, fuck that you better hit that shit!"

"I'm good bro" I replied

"If you don't hit that again we about to beat yo ass! Quit acting soft boy and hit that shit."

And soooooooo... I did, I took another massive blast of Mother Nature and if I was high before now I was LOW, low like in hell shaking hands with Lucifer himself and running in quicksand while being chased by a million hungry goblins and spooks. And if I thought that was the end of it, the homie pulling me up outta my chair kicked it into 6th gear and high as FUCK I fell back into my chair.

"Come on man, get yo ass up! It's time to go! We gotta get back to school!"

THE SCHOOL!? These niggas must be crazy, I thought to myself, I was out past Pluto and they were talking about getting to school! I stood up anyway, slow as it might have been, ha-ha, each step weighted and an extreme effort. Finally, a little empathy came from one of the homies "What's up bro? Nigga you good!?"

"Yeah, I'm coo my nigga" I lied. And he knew it because he wrapped my arm around his shoulder and helped me down the stairs. It was only 3 blocks or so back to the school but it seemed like eternity. When we finally did arrive back and I made my way to class my talk with god had already begun. As I sat at my desk, slumped over the desk with my eyes closed I started praying and making all kinds of promises to my savior

"Please god, don't let me die, I swear I will NEVER smoke again, just don't let me die, don't let this shit kill me!" BWAAHAAAHAAAA… Everything in the room was spinning, the room itself was spinning and I felt like I was sinking into a deep dark tunnel. Wobbling as I stood up I made my way outside hoping that fresh air would help me I made it up the stairs miraculously and when I did I just laid down over the top of the railing and hugged it for dear life. At this point, FUCK what Galileo said, the universe was Zackery-centric and BOY was it spinning around me! Just when I thought it couldn't get any worse. Mr. Green, Franklin's school security guard was hovering RIGHT over me. Fortunately I was able to lie my way out of that situation but Karma has a way of biting you in the ass. A few days later I was expelled for fighting in the hallways. I was on the road to nowhere fast, the only thing that I had going for me in school was football. I LOVED football, it was the only thing that I remember being good at and praised for at that time of my Life. It was fun, I got to punch, tackle, and crack the shit out of people without getting into any trouble and as aggressive as I was I excelled in the sport. It was a channel for my boy-child energy and what more for the pain I was experiencing watching my mother be beaten. I remember even from a young age playing football was my high, it didn't matter if I played line, full back or middle linebacker. I was a beast! My record was dope! Full of tackles, sacks and even some defensive touchdowns and a safety, my team Loved me, the coaches Loved me, I felt seen, when I was on the field I was in control and I was a champion but with the expulsion, even that was taken from me.

It seemed as if that was the pattern in my Life, my father was taken from me, my mother found a place called Big Brothers that gave kids without dads a mentor/father figure and I had THREE, but every time I got close to one they abandoned me too, my grandpa who was like my father married a Colombian woman and moved to Florida on me, so it was only my mom I had left because me and my little brother didn't really get along either and she too inevitably turned her back on me. When she got married to her boyfriend and he bought us all a house to move into together again I felt like the last person I had, the last thing in the world was taken from me. So fuck it, I started running away from my "home". I parenthesize home, because even that felt like a place I wasn't welcomed or a place that I could let my guard down and just be myself. After we moved and my mom's boyfriend became her husband, his son started living with us too and shit got real strict and fucked up anyways which made running away even more appealing-I mean who wants to get whipped and stand in the cold on a day to day basis- Once we all moved in together it seemed like spending time at home consisted solely of doing chores or getting ready to go to church, yea we lived in the household where Monday through Saturday our parents would do as they please but ya ass was definitely going to church! Not once but TWICE on Sunday AND depending on how moms felt, WEDNESDAYS SOMETIMES TOO! This wasn't your everyday normal church either, let me tell YOU, it was some OTHER shit! I mean STRANGE! If you don't know what Apostolic Pentecostal means just be HAPPY for yourself! I mean you walk into the doors and people are SCREAMING, JUMPING, RUNNING around and ROLLING ON THE FLOOR "SPEAKING IN TONGUES"! The first time you see this it is SCAREY! Man I ain't even going to front, the first few times I went I was nervous and SPOOKED! I mean people were jumping up and down and the ministers in the church would put their hands on people and they would just fall down also there was so much crying and screaming. People sounded like they were being hurt while they were… Praising god? It was so weird and confusing to me when I first came into the church at 9 or 10 years old. I didn't know what to make of it all but eventually though beside all of its oddities it wore on me. Between the people wanting to give me hugs, and how they smiled at me every time they saw me and when I could quote a short Bible verse being awarded with candy and recognition it felt great and so I dived into it myself, ha-ha. I mean, I really dove into it, I started attending the school, I started memorizing Bible verses even participating on the Bible Quizzing TEAM, I even gave a couple mini sermons, and had the ENTIRE church up on their feet clapping and shouting amen! I think when you're young even though it is being forced upon you or maybe because it is being forced upon you, you just want to be a part of something so bad that you will try ANYTHING and find something to like about it or possibly even just make yourself start liking it but there's also a very real draw to religion on an intellectual, emotional and spiritual level as well that first PULLS you in and then propels you to get deeper into the religion especially if you experienced trauma that created codependency and the need to find self-worth outside of yourself but that's a whole other book by itself. So, long story short I got sucked into the religion and there even came a point where I had the opportunity to go to the school in the church when I was around 8-9, and shit, after being stuck inside that damn insane asylum they were calling a school I jumped at the opportunity. I mean really just being that there was finally girls in class with me was enough for me to want to go to the private school but also there was a familiarity with the students and teachers from going to church with them and the idea of closeness and connection sounded so great. I wanted that more than anything.

Anyway, the point of me bringing up the church was that it was there I met another one of its hostages (I recollect telling my mom I'm sick to try and get out of having to go to church just for her to say "That's when you need Jesus the most, you need to go to church son so that the pastor can anoint you with oils and pray for you that Jesus will heal your body!" mind you every time she felt ill she'd just drop us off in the front, if even that. She'd make us take the bus most of the time... SMH.) But me and the other church P.O.W. (Prisoner Of War) would chill in the back and chop it up, one of the best things about church was ALL of the girls! God DAMN! There were HELLA ladies in the church and dressed their best! With their long beautiful hair and their dresses or skirts on. There were times if for nothing else, to see the girls was why I would go and sit down on the pew for a couple hours at a time! They separated us younger people, we had to sit in the front and girls on one side and boys on the other. Of course I had no problem turning my neck to see what was going on over on the other side or should I say what was bouncing around when the girls I thought were cute were jumping to praise the Lord. There were a few times when the pastor called me out for that as well. I was a little pervert and there is no telling how many times I got caught rubber necking to admire the church girls across the aisle from me. Knowing me you know I had a crush on EACH and EVERY single one of them. They all looked good, BUT there was this ONE, she was gorgeous, could sing amazingly and had already began her life as a "Back Sliding Sinner" I could tell by the brief conversations we had but at that time I was only 9 years old and she was a teenager so she wasn't really giving me play. I actually remember hearing her sing a Missy Elliott song, that one that said "if you gotta big dick let me search it, find out how hard I gotta work it" I got all excited and was like oh shit she's about that Life so I said Hey I know that song and sang it with her and then asked her if she knew the Luda song "I wanna li-li-li-lick you from your head to your toes" she DID and we sang THAT one together and she even did her little hip "gyration" (as the elders of the church would call it) dance as we sang it and I was so confident that she was into me and I just blurted out will you be my girlfriend (Gosh I had no finesse or ANYTHING back then hahaha) and she smiled and said we can't....Yeah that was Brooke--------

SO we would chop it up me and the other P.O.W. at the church but conversation never got too deep however when I ran away I hit the homie up and sure enough he let me crash with him. He was older than me, around 19, and I was still 15 at the time this story took place. Long story short my P.O.W. friend was a rider, and a few steps ahead of me off the porch. It wasn't but the 2nd night I stayed at his house he asked me if I have ever robbed someone before and I said no, he asked me if I was down to and it was a wrap, I had said yes and the 2nd night on the streets I went and robbed a convenience store with him just down the street from his place. At that age it was the WILDEST shit I had ever done! Talk about adrenaline rush! However I would have known right then and there to stop with crime if I was as wise as I am now because I was in Love with the GAME the GLAMOUR of it all and not the DOLLAR which was my FIRST mistake! I know now that the saying DONT GET

66

HIGH OFF YOUR OWN SUPPLY is relatable to all aspects of business. And in this sense the magnitude of how game struck I was inevitably would not be beneficial for being IN the game because it didn't allow for clarity and the precision that it would take to plan and execute strategies with cunning, objectiveness and non-attachment it takes to really get far in anti-social entrepreneurship. The thrill I felt that night wouldn't last the length of the 28 months I'd later spend incarcerated on my 90 month sentence let alone the span of my life being labeled not just a felon at 15, but a violent one at that.

There was a lot that led up to me voluntarily telling the police I robbed a store at gunpoint. As I said, when me, my little brother and my mother started living with her husband and his son shit didn't just get strict shit got real. Real abusive that is. You didn't clean the bathroom thoroughly enough you did push-ups till you began to hyperventilate and if you stopped or dropped to the floor when your muscles fatigued then you got your ass whooped. Sure, there was the traditional belt to the ass and wherever it landed but there was a brush, a fist, a backhand, other miscellaneous objects etc. Example, I remember having to military crawl through a sawdust pit as my mother's husband yelled as loud as he could not even 6 inches from my ear as he pulled my pants down and filled my draws with sawdust, other times I was made to stand in our backyard for hours in the snow wearing only my underpants and tennis shoes or in the same whether being hosed down like a wild beast cause I showered for 7 minutes instead of the 5 minute military showers he was used to! After that I felt like being made to eat dog food at the threat of more abusive violence was no big deal, I would rather eat the dog food then feel the bludgeoning of a fist or the sting of a belt against my skin. These atrocities were the daily abuse I lived with regularly. They wounded and scarred my ego and my spirit. Not just my body. They made me timid and afraid to speak my mind and being that my mother sat by and watched me being abused if not participating in it herself, the one and only person who I trusted and had not yet betrayed me I developed deep seeded trust issues and a story in my mind that told me constantly I could not speak up for myself. These just to name two of the problems this abuse created. As I grew I eventually got a little bolder and a little braver, when I crossed paths in the hallway with Chris my mother's husband Instead of hugging the wall and getting out of the way to let him pass I squared my shoulders off and purposefully bumped into him. It was small, but it was all I could do in my subtle way of saying slowly but surely I am finding my voice and one day I will not only stand up to you but I will turn the tables! However with all of the trauma and fear that was alive in me still it would be a while until I could truly stand up for myself fully but in the meantime we would have pushing matches that ended in him hitting me or my mother screaming for us to stop.

On one day, a day that would change the rest of my Life I had been helping clean his bike shop, it was just after noon and I was asked to go get lunch for him, my mother and myself. I went to get the food and came back hungry, mouth watering and ready to eat. I gave them their food and sat down to eat mine as they dug into theirs just before I heard Chris once again yelling at me in his trademark condescending tone.

"You don't get to eat yet! You have to vacuum before you get to eat!"

Now in my mind I thought DAMN, their eating I've been cleaning all day, I'm hungry I just want to eat, shit I just went and got them their food in the first place and they are eating in front of me! For him to tell me I can't eat just isn't fair!

"What!?" I retorted

"What did I tell you about what'ing me!? Don't what me! You need to VACUUM before you EAT!"

"Man I am HUNGRY! I will vacuum right after I eat."

"You're going to do what the fuck I tell you to do and do it NOW!" he said as he got off his chair posturing.

Fear swiftly gripped me and began to once again paralyze not just my voice but also my body but- "FUCK YOU!" I said as I too got off my chair and we clashed yet again, however, this time unbeknownst to me would be different, much different. My mom jumped in between us as our fists flew through the air, halting are physical violence momentarily but the rain of verbal assaults continued to fly back and forth at one another. I was so tired of being picked on, bullied, disrespected, and made to feel less than. I just wanted for him to feel some of the pain he had caused me, I wanted to hurt him and I wanted to make him feel the entire weight of it spanned over the last 5 years. I wanted to punish him, yet my fear and my mother stood in the way. I felt defeated. Not wanting to hurt her and fear still being very much alive inside of me I allowed her to wrestle my half responsive body to a back room as I tried to get out of her grasp without injuring her. She began to grow tired and knowing that when she did the only thing stopping me and Chris was space and opportunity as he antagonized me from the front room…. My mother yelled for him to call the police on me and of course his bitch ass did. My body fully numb now, I froze, just stood there silently looking into my mother's eyes frantically hoping this was for pretend, that she would say never mind, that she would smile or show any sign of Love to me. She was my savior she wouldn't, she couldn't… Not to me…

Reality set back in as I heard Chris talking to the dispatch officer. "Hang up the phone you fucking coward! You're a fucking snitch!" I yelled at him, "Quit being a fucking mark ass bitch and fight me!" All 370lbs of my mother was now on top of me and holding me down as I struggled and squirmed to get free but the truth be told had I gotten free I was too scared to actually fight with him, I just wanted to be heard, I just wanted to be seen. I wanted my pain to be validated. He probably could have just given me a hug and said he was sorry and let me kick him in his shin or punch his belly and I would have been okay.

All I wanted was to matter. Shortly later the police had arrived and I could hear my own mother telling them to get me out of here as two officers kept me quarantined away off in the room my mother had held me in. She asked them to take me away but they could not, no law had been broken by me in fact the only one at fault was Chris for putting his hands on a minor. But wait…

"If you really want him gone you could say he interfered with a 911 call"-

"But he didn't" I heard my mother rebuttal.

"Well I am just saying that's one way we could get him taken into custody".

… Silence….

"Okay, yea, fine, whatever, he interfered with the 911 call" my mother said.

My heart sank into my gut, the woman who VOWED to Love me and protect me was now not only working with the police against me but lying on me too to get me arrested, handcuffed, thrown in the back of a squad car and hauled away. My whole entire existence, reality and being was shaken, my world was shattered. I had been betrayed by my LAST and ONLY ally, no one Loved me, no one cared about me, and I felt WORTHLESS! I was neglected and abandoned and REJECTED by the same woman who birthed me and made a promise to always hold me. I was left in the lowest states of confusion, depression and despair. I had no one. My fear of being alone had finally came to fruition, I was lonely, shackled and being held captive in the back of a cop car a lost black child on my way to become counted amongst the herd of statistics. This was the first day of the rest of my Life that I would be labeled no longer a child even though I wasn't an adult, no longer a high school student although I was in class the day before, but at the age of 15 years old I'd be labeled a dangerous adult felon. When we got to the station I was asked a series of routine questions and over the feeling devastated and just feeling numb I thought to myself just being me had gotten me nowhere, No one, not even my own mother liked me I just wanted to be accepted, I wanted to be wanted.

The lady screening me asked "Have you ever used or possessed a firearm"

I wanted to be seen in the worst way, ANY WAY, I was tired of everyone around me except me receiving all of the attention…

"Yes."

"Excuse me?" It was now my turn, shit what's the worst that could happen? They send me to a foster home? No one at my own home Loves me anyway.

"I said, yes, I have used a gun. I robbed a store a few weeks ago." The poor woman looked confused as a redneck at a spelling bee.

"Are you sure?" She asked leaning in. WOW! Yes, I finally had someone's attention, someone was noticing me, and it even felt a little powerful playing a "tough guy".

"Yea man, check the shit out. I am sure the cops were called. It was the market on 92nd and Holgate across the street from the AM/PM" I said acting as hardened as I could. Right then and there she got up and disappeared. She must have called the precinct for the area where the market was located and checked out my statement with local detectives because she came back with a serious face and asked me how I knew about this robbery and I responded because I did it. She then asked me to go into a holding cell and informed me that 2 detectives were on their way and that she hopes I wasn't lying because this was serious. And as the door slammed shut with the metallic clank and echo in the cold sterile room I was now trapped in I felt even lonelier. The severity and just how serious this entire situation was then beginning to really sink in on me.

I sat in the room for what seemed like 8 hours, on cold concrete hard dirty tile floor, just me, myself and my thoughts. When detective Benniga finally opened the door it didn't matter to me he was there to incarcerate me for the rest of my juvenile Life, I was just relieved to see that door open and have some form of human interaction after staring at brick and metal for hours. He told me it was unusual for someone to just randomly confess to such a serious crime and asked me if someone put me up to it. Still feeling worthless and not knowing how to just state that and say I want to be seen, I want to MATTER, I want to be cared about but knowing this was getting me attention even if negative I went ahead and maintained my story. He said I'd be looking at, at least 90 months in prison, but at 15 that had no bearing in my mind. It didn't even register at all. He said I would be charged as an adult, I had no idea what the justice system was let alone how it leveraged punitive justice against even children of color to perpetuate the new Jim Crow and to continue thriving in making big bucks for those who profited from the prison industrial complex. He said turn around and put your hands behind your back and now only at 15 unfortunately I was already familiar with those words and I did as he said.

I remember driving to the jail and my mother oddly enough being in the parking lot. She yelled from her car "Do not tell them anything else! Keep your mouth shut!" I was so scared that even seeing the same person who had earlier betrayed our bond and asked for the police to be called on me in the first place actually lifted my spirits but it also tugged them hard in the opposite direction as well.

I remember going into booking and the old white haired woman who was so sweet seeing my young face and asking if I had got caught shop lifting. I told her I was being brought in on 2 counts of Armed Robbery. One count in the first degree and the other in the 2nd. I remember her looking at me with disbelief. Looking into my eyes and seeing my innocence and even asking me what happened? You didn't really rob a store did you? She couldn't believe that I had the capacity to do that and her intuition was right I had not technically robbed any store nor do I think that I would have been capable of pulling that off. She told me that I wouldn't be held in this cage for long because I was only 15 and obviously just at the wrong place at the wrong time. Essentially I was young and innocent. The woman than called a male guard down to booking. This was the first time in my life that I would ever do what I was about to do in fact it was the first time in my LIFE after I was molested that I got naked in front of another human being let alone being forced to do so. First I was asked to get undressed, I took all of my clothes off besides my underwear feeling insecure getting naked in front of another human being, he said that I had to take my underpants off as well or that I would stay in this holding tank and not be fed. So with long hesitation I finally took off the last of my protective garments and stood fully exposed to this grown man. He asked me to lift my hands in the air so he could see my armpits. He asked me to run my hands through my hair to make sure I was hiding nothing in my hair. He asked me to open my mouth wide and stick out my tongue and to run my fingers through the space where my cheeks touched my teeth and my gums to ensure nothing was concealed there neither. He then told me to lift up my scrotum. After this I was instructed to turn around so he could see my back, lift up each of my feet to ensure nothing was under them and the most humiliating part of it all for me was when he told me to bend over and spread my ass cheeks exposing my asshole to him and then to squat and cough. When I was finished I couldn't unglue my eyes from the ground, I was feeling so much embarrassment and I was ashamed. I was given a wristband to be identified with and the grey uniform that would blend me into the sea of other children being housed like animals inside of DELH (Donald E. Long Home). I was housed in Alpha Unit that night and it was definitely a fitting unit to be housed in because it was the first night of my Life living in this new hell that I would learn a lot more about as the years drifted by.

I was the youngest on my unit when they transferred me to Bravo 2 where they housed all of the prisoners with Measure 11 cases. Measure 11 was a measure passed in Oregon that if you committed any person to person violent crime regardless if you were 15 or 55 you would be charged as an adult and serve a mandatory minimum prison sentence with no good time, no earned time, no anything but barbed wire and concrete walls for the entirety of your stay in the department of corrections and the lowest amount of time that you were sentenced with if charged with a measure 11 crime was 5 years. Five years FLAT. It is hard to think that people actually passed this law into existence. To think that there were people that wanted anyone let alone 15, 16, and 17 year old kids to spend at least a 3rd of their Life contained within a cage. What I realized later in life was that the language around the bill was so difficult to decipher to most of the community that they thought they were voting for children to mandatorily receive the minimum sentence possible. When I got to the unit I thought to myself once again through the lens of my conditioned mind that these were the cool people, the boys from the hood and in the music videos with hella homies and girls and tons of money so I wanted to be accepted, I tried to fit in. I tried to walk, talk and act like a "Gangsta" but I think my voice was still a little too high and my smile a little too bright. I remember sitting down with two brothers playing dominoes and saying "Lemme get next Cuzz."

"What!? The fuck you just say crab ass nigga!?" Before I even knew what had happened DING DING Round 1... I was scared as shit and took the L on that one, I ain't even gonna front. I was nowhere near ready for the culture that I had found myself spontaneously dumped into.

I remember telling another guy "Shut up bitch!" That was round 2 DING DING! Another L. I was quickly learning that Life on this side of the fence wasn't a game, these guys weren't playing, it wasn't the glamorous cool shit I saw on music videos and thought about when I thought of being a Gang Member there was pain and fear, hatred, and the constant threat of violence was real and dangerous and brought out the PTSD in me from watching my mother be beaten and also being the target of my step father's abuse. This shit was hard. I gave into my fear once again and allowed myself to become a victim. Thankfully there wasn't any rape in my county experience but the pain of being physically and verbally assaulted cut very deep, being bullied made me feel so weak and powerless, however as we all know what doesn't kill you makes you stronger or in my case angrier and more alienated from my true self. In hindsight I think that it was those times that prepared me to be able to accept and embrace the mental and spiritual anguish I would face later in Life. And be able to bounce back from it somewhat gracefully. All of my fights weren't losses, I beat up one guy that came into my room and two other guys that thought they were gonna jump me. I have realized sense then that I am actually a decent fighter but I was afraid of violence due to all the trauma I had endured, it triggered the memories from the past. I'll let you make sense of that.

I remember when I was sent to Coffee Creek I was FINISHED! The days of being bullied were OVER (plus there was the very real fear in my mind that if I didn't stand up for myself being that I was in an adult prison now that I would be made into someone's bitch and be raped and I definitely did not want that to happen)! It was the very first time I ate a meal in DOC's custody. I got my tray, filled my cup and went and sat down at a table that had no one at it and started to eat my food. Eventually a couple other dudes sat down and said "Hey youngster someone sits there." They had no aggression in their voice or body language not even an attitude, but, of course as scared as I was and not wanting to be any ones bitch I perceived a threat and thought they were trying to Punk me for my seat.

"WHAT!?"

"That is someone's seat."

"I ain't moving for NOBODY, whoever seat it is if he wants it he is gonna have to beat my ass if he wants it back!" I won't lie, my heart was beating faster than a mother fucker in my throat but I knew I at least had to front like I wasn't afraid and could stand up for myself on my own two feet.

The guys that had sat down at the table just kind of shook their heads and smirked it off and I went back to eating scared as shit that I was about to get in a fight with some grown ass man and get beat up. Across the way I saw this white guy lift his cup up in the air and make eye contact with me and then he nodded his head over towards the fountain drinks telling me to meet him over there. I grabbed my cup and marched over to the fountain as stoically and tough as I could.

"Hey youngster I saw what just went down, this is your first time down huh? Those guys weren't trying to punk you, we all just sit with guys we know its protocol. That tough guy shit will draw you unwanted attention, really this isn't even the place to do that, this is classification and so everyone is trying to be on their best. If we were already upstate that would have started a fight if not a riot just be careful youngster you don't have nothing to prove to nobody. I think there's a table with cowboy that just opened up he's the big black dude over there from C.R.I.P. I'll introduce yall. How old are you anyway?"

"I'm 16"

"Fuck man what the hell are you even doin' in here? Just be chill and get out of here, save that tough shit for when you hit the yard"

I don't really got much to say about the time between being released from prison and getting locked back up again because all I did was the same dumb shit that got me locked up in the first place, that is fall back into the limitations and boxes of the stereotypes constructed by the powers that keep this system of oppression running on the backs of us people of color and those who are economically poor as we are being exploited. I have to admit I was in a state of ignorance. You see, being born black and poor I was given a choice. I could be a gang member, a drug dealer, a jack boy and/or a pimp all of which are identities that were supported by the television, music, movies and therefore society as a whole because, yeah, we mirror back what it is we have seen or been told. No matter black or white, when living unconsciously and without the skill of critically thinking, well, monkey see… monkey do. So, my two options, I could float where EVERYTHING pointed for me to go, the path of least resistance that actually pulled me towards drug use, crime and a lifestyle that tore my soul, or I could go rogue and challenge not just the system or "The Man" if you would but even my very own people, the people that looked like me but because they too had been trained to uphold the status quo that kept the 1% living luxuriously with power and privilege through the social conditioning of mass media they too also would combat this path with their animosity and resentment which normally sounded like comments such as "what you think you're too good for us?" Or "Why you always reading and shit and be sounding like a white boy." Or simply making me a target because if you were not talking shit and pretending you were hard then obviously you must be soft and not capable of defending yourself or standing up for what you believe in, RIGHT? FUCK NO! That is the stupidest shit that I have ever believed in but because it is supported everywhere we look we grow up believing it to be true. And I have to admit I fell right into the trap. I let Suga Free, Mac Dre and Messy Marv become the prophets of my religion instead of my entertainment and allowed myself to be carried away into a land where I made their lyrics my reality and measured my manhood according to how many of the things I could do that they talked about in their songs. Don't forget the peer pressure and the agenda I thought that friends had for me which really was only created in my head. I didn't know that they too were just as cornered with their back to the wall or traumatized as I was because god forbid we spoke to each other about REAL shit. That wouldn't be "gangsta"... I did nothing but perpetuate the stereotypical norms of black men the short time I was out between Youth Authority and DOC and since we all know what that looks like already I feel no need to talk about it. In fact, you can pick up a Terry Woods, Eric Jerome Dickey or any of that other lit that perpetuates our oppression and the stereotypical bullshit that glorifies Life in the streets and our Queens as sex objects if you're looking for entertainment. I ain't that nigga. I'm gon lace you and support you in getting' Game Tight and Gorgeous. AND, know that I believe reading period even if it isn't the best material is still reading and exercises your mind. MANDATORY! In fact, it was the two authors I mentioned that I was reading before I stepped up my book game and it was Dickeys overwhelmingly vivid imagination that I resorted back to when I needed to take a break from the hardcore laborious studying I was doing which was the reset button for me to be able to get back into the heavy mental lifting. But more to that later, it comes further on in my story after some bumps and bruises...

Growing up I had no intention of being a "pimp" I put the parenthesis there because despite what KOIN or KATU has to say I never truly saw myself as a pimp even when I did boast or brag about having women who were selling their bodies for my own ignorant and greedy capitalistic conquest. I remember actually feeling resentment for pimping being that it was what my mother always reminded me my runaway father's occupation was. And yet it was glamorized all over mainstream culture to the point where even people who had never even heard of the blade or checkin' a trap were using the word pimp and pimpin' all the time! Pimp my ride, what's up pimpin', its big pimpin spending G's... Pimpin became sensationalized. I remember when my girlfriend told me she had done some hoeing I felt a knot in my stomach and tension rise from my chest into my neck. I remember feeling sad and feeling her pain and my own anger swell up that somehow this beautiful woman had been a victim to sexual exploitation. I would have NEVER in a million years thought that I would be behind her being sexually exploited in only a few short months after she had shared that vulnerable and still tender experience she had lived through.

I had met Brooke in the church many years ago. She was pretty even back then and she sang like an angel. I had a crush on her but being that I was the chubby 9 year old church boy and she was a beautiful teenage girl already looking outside of the church for her excitement I wasn't much of a candidate myself for her as a crush. Nonetheless, that didn't stop me. Every time I saw her whether it be in school, the church or out and about I ALWAYS would flirt with Brooke. She would smile and deflect of course but she was just so intriguing to me that I couldn't stop my flirtatious ways. At that time I had already learned to flirt and wanted to be around girls all the time. Wanted to learn about woman and how they saw things. I remember reading girly magazines just to try and figure out how these beautiful beings thought and how to make myself more attractive to them. Brooke never did give me the time of day back then and it wasn't long before she left the church altogether being pressured by the puritan-like community to conform to their ways and definitely was an outcast when she became pregnant. I didn't see her much after she left the church. She was considered a back slider after she left our congregation and we would pray for her every now and again hoping that god would direct her back onto the path of the "righteous" but if you were not living your life according to how the pastor saw fit the church was definitely not a place you wanted to be. The judgements and scorn mixed with your own shame and guilt because you had been conditioned since you were birthed to believe that the path you were on is the only true path causes so much pain when your spirit doesn't resonate with sitting in the pews any more being passive and yielding to the status quo.

So why does all of this matter when I started talking about being a "pimp"… Well when I got out of prison at 17 years old I was no longer the 9 year old cute little chubby boy. In fact, I was about 6ft tall and had put on some muscle mass and taken on the stereotypical look of what you might call a "bad boy". And due to social media it wasn't long until I was surprised by receiving a message from Brooke in my inbox on Myspace. I couldn't respond fast enough! The girl I had crushed on for several years of my young Life was now attracted to me. Ahhh, it started off all so innocent, I talked her into meeting at the church and we stayed late after service talking just catching up and shooting the shit. Eventually after getting past the small talk and casual conversation we started going deep. Staying up all night long talking till we fell asleep on the phone and sharing intimate details and experiences of our Lives. It was during one of these late night phone calls that Brooke shared with me her experience as a prostitute. It hurt, hearing she had sold her body cut deep into my being as I empathized with the pain she was exhibiting reflecting on that story from her past. I remember trying to comfort and support her as she told me her stories and telling her that I despised that lifestyle and the men that were a part of it. Not knowing that just right around the corner I too would be no freer of sin then the people I was condemning.

My mother did not like Brooke but I was in Love so when she told me that I had to make a choice between continuing to see Brooke and finding shelter under her roof I chose to continue to be with Brooke. Not even 6 months had passed since I was released from prison and I was now homeless and without a job. I didn't have anywhere to go. The last time I was placed in this situation I ended up catching an armed robbery charge and spending precious time incarcerated. I had to come up with a plan fast. I didn't know much about ecstasy but I did know that it would be one of the easiest drugs to sell being that it came in pill form and didn't need to be weighed or bagged up. I also knew from the stories that Brooke had told me from the past few years I had missed as we caught up that she had a plug on the Thizz and a client base that she had had nights where she would dump an entire roll in a night. Being broke and without really having a place to stay that didn't sound like such a bad idea so I began to set my intention on the bezel game. The only problem though was I had about $400 to my name but no plug and when I asked Brooke to look into it she couldn't find anyone that was on either. Being in the pinch that I was I took that last bit of money I had and on a whim went up to Seattle to meet up with someone I had just heard through the grapevine could put me on with 100 pills for the 3. For me that would be good because it would mean that if I sold each pill for at least $10 would make about $700 profit. Albeit it never goes dollar for dollar like that in the street yet on the other hand if you have superb hustle skills you can bend corners and bust moves that will equal it all up or better. Problem is when we got up to Seattle the connect started playing games talking about he was busy and was trying to get to me but had people who wanted to cop more weight than the one roll from him that I was trying to get so they were first priority. Stressed the fuck out I went for the okie doke and went to meet with some guys a girl I had known from up that way connected me with. We drove from Seattle to Kent to meet these dudes and when we pulled up they asked where the money was, I asked where the work was and they gave me a bag of pills. Not being familiar with X I accepted the bag and gave them the money I had brought up. Being that we stayed the night in a hotel the night before I now only had about $340 left to my name. I was nervous yet I was excited I had finally got my hands on some pills and would now be able to make some money and I had big dreams of flippin' these pills and getting on for real. Silk, one of Brooke's friends asked to see the pills and hesitantly I handed them over to him. He took one look at the bag of pills and said "Nigga, this ain't not damn Thizz!" My heart dropped right down into my belly. I had been fooled and the last of my money stolen from me! I asked what do we do and he said call them back and tell them you want your money back so I did and Brooke turned the car around. We went back to the apartment we had met these dudes at and I started blowing up their phone as we parked in front of their building. I also asked Silk to pass me his burner and cocked it back as soon as I had it in my hands. I was pissed the fuck off and feeling so powerless! The

LAST of my money was gone and all I had was some fake E bombs! These muh fuckas had me fucked up. Finally, I got ahold of one of the guys that was with the guy who sold me the pills. I asked him to go get his friend that had my money and that I didn't want this shit. He went into an apartment to go talk to his friend. Another man came to talk to me and saw that I had a blapper on me and asked me about it. I just denied having anything on me and he went into the apartment that the other two were in.

I remember seeing the three of them coming out a few minutes later and I could see the outlines of what I am guessing were MP5s and an UZI. Only thing I had was this damn .22 pistol I had grabbed from Silk. I was outgunned, 200 miles from home and I had my girlfriend in the car with me. Between that and the fear itself I was feeling from the weaponry I saw them carrying I decided I had no interest in picking this as any battle of mine. I told Brooke lets go and we got on the road back towards Portland. I was homeless, no job and only had $40 to my name...

I had to come up with something quick. I asked Brooke if she wanted to go to the beach the next day after we had got back to Portland knowing she would say yes, being that it was her favorite place to get away to. The entire ride I was charming. I knew enough to know that I needed to be sweet and kind if I was going to ask her to stretch outside of what had now became comfortable with. When we got to the beach we walked the coast where the water licked up the beach tickling the sand as waves reached up the shore. Knowing it was my only chance I held her hand and made her feel special while inside of myself I was scared and wrestling with what I was thinking to propose to her. Eventually being stuck in a mindset of scarcity and not only being afraid of poverty and homelessness but just never having shit and wanting to see some stacks I decided that I would ask my girlfriend the woman that I Loved if she would do something I had at once despised and that was to hoe again. I explained to her that I just needed her to get enough money for me to get some drugs I could sell and then I would take care of the rest. I remember her looking me in my eyes and asking me if I wanted her to have sex with other men. I sincerely told her that I didn't want her to fuck anyone and I damn sure didn't want her sucking nobody else's dick so she synthesized the idea of giving back massages that ended in hand jobs. It was a compromise but it felt a whole lot better than her having sex or wrapping her lips around another man's dick. We agreed that she would give erotic massages and we went back to Portland. When we got back she set up a CL account and ad giving me a quick tutorial on how to do it because personally she hated having to post her own ads. I didn't feel like I was very good at it either but I decided to do it anyway. It was the least I could do as she had agreed to sell her body so I could get on. I remember the first call she received. It was an outcall to a condo downtown. I was hella nervous, I really didn't even want her to do this for her safety, not wanting to share her, and fear of it being illegal I was a bundle of nerves! When I saw her dress up and do her hair and makeup I even felt a tinge of jealousy because I had never had the privilege of her getting all dolled up for me. It was a very awkward feeling. I remember her catching a little bit of an attitude but eventually after talking for a while and her expressing her frustration with the whole situation and my insistence she decided to go up to the apartment we were parked in front of and take on the date. Almost as soon as she stepped out of the car and was out of my sight I was skeptical of whether or not I had made the right decision and I was scared.

With every minute that passed by my boiling point was closer and closer. I got so concerned and worried about her as the hour passed by that she was scheduled for that I called her phone continuously and started walking around the building trying to find a way in. Not even realizing I didn't know the unit number that she was in. Finally she called me and asked ME if I was alright! HA! I told her I was worried sick about her and she had a hell of a poker face because she not only made me calm down but she also made me believe that she didn't mind doing this. She even bragged about it which along with how desensitized to sex in of itself I already was lowered my internal barriers to engaging in the sex industry in this way.

The next few days were pretty much a blur. Wake up, find some breakfast, post an ad, get a call, leave the room, count the money, get drunk and high, repeat. Sometimes we would throw in a hotel party and some pills if we were really feeling ourselves but that was essentially the Life we were living. Where there is one there is usually two. In our case there were three. Being in Portland we inevitably ran into some of Brooke's friends who also had women getting money for them. In fact, it was Silk and another cat named Nubius. These cats were in their later 20s and I won't front they seemed cool enough and I began to look up to them which is amusing when I think about it now because they was complimenting the shit I had, staring at my girl and asking me for rides when they needed to get somewhere because they didn't have a car of their own. Speaking of which it was IN my car while we were outside of the Motel 6 because each of our girls had an in-call at the same time. So here we were in my Cadillac passing a blunt around crackin' jokes and shit and this joker Silk says "Ay man, haha, we like the 3 musketeers of pimpin!"

"Man what the fuck!? You crazy as shit ain't nobody no god damn 3 fuckin musketeers and I ain't no fuckin pimp either!" I said defending my girlfriend and feeling somewhat offended personally.

"What the fuck is you then while you got your girl up there turnin' a trick and bout to break bread soon as you step in the door?"

"She ain't in there fuckin nobody she ain't a hoe! That's my girl!"

"What you think she in there doing then?"

"She giving the trick a back massage and might jack the nigga off or something!"

"You mean to tell me this whole time she ain't been fuckin or suckin' no dick?"

"Naw man she ain't doing that shit, she's my girl."

"Wow. What the fuck your missing hella paper! Why don't you have her fucking these tricks?"

"Cause that's my girl I Love her man. I don't want her fuckin on no other dudes."

"What you Love more, her or money?"

"I Love her homie"

"Man for real that sounds like some simp shit, you can't tell me you love her more than you love this paper"

"Shit, I guess I Love the money more than her." I felt pressured to say.

"Man you need to tell that bitch hoe up or blow up! Tell her you want her to start fuckin so yall can start getting some real paper!" ....

As I directed Brooke to sit down on the steps of the stairway at motel 6 I saw the curiosity in her face and eyes. I was processing all of the information that Silk had just told me as I nervously asked him questions about this very moment just minutes ago. "What happens if she doesn't wanna do it?" "Nigga she Love you she will literally do ANYTHING for you right now!"

I assured her that I appreciated everything she had been doing for us and that although it has been good we needed more. "Just be blunt and say what the fuck you want." I told her I needed her to start fucking some of these tricks... Her face screwed up as pain, betrayal, shame, dread and anger all welled up to the surface as she took in my request. "I FUCKIN KNEW IT! I KNEW THAT AS SOON AS I STARTED THIS IS THE FUCKING SHIT THAT WOULD HAPPEN! ARE YOU SERIOUSLY ASKING ME TO FUCK OTHER PEOPLE!? NO! NO, I'M NOT SOME FUCKING HOE! I CAN'T BELIEVE YOU!" She stood up to walk away and I grabbed her saying that I don't want this either and it wouldn't be long. She pulled herself away from my grasp and I let her go, watching her walk away and head back to the hotel room we were staying in. Truly I didn't want it. Even when she was just giving erotic massages a piece of me left with her every time she went on a call and when she came back that piece of my soul unfortunately never did. I was caught in the cross-fire of a battle that was commissioned long ago. A war being waged on my mind, body and spirit every day without even one idea of what was going on. Fed into poverty for the exploitation of capitalism due to my race and my economical background. The music I was "supposed" to listen to, the t.v. shows I was "supposed" to watch, the lack of education I was intended to receive, the stress I was intended to encounter from police staring at me, grocers following me, people walking to the other side of the street when they saw me coming, the complete alienation of self and then the shaming when I spoke up about it. Not having shit your whole Life made doing things you would never do and don't even want to do a lot more attractive no matter the cost.

I went back into the room scared that I was going to lose the woman I Loved just wanting to hug her and tell her how sorry I was for even suggesting that she would sell her precious body. I just wanted to support her and Love on her and with the hope of lots of money being on the other side of her selling herself when I didn't even have a place to stay let alone money to my name and the socially constructed idea of masculinity stomping around in my mind yelling at me I felt challenged to stick with what I had suggested. If she says no just pack your shit up and leave. She Loves you bro she isn't going to let this separate you. It might be a couple hours or it might be a couple days but if you leave and don't say nothing to her till she says yes, she will say yes. I hopped into the shower and then took my time in picking out my best outfit and made sure it was something she liked than I began to pack up my clothes into my suitcase. I could feel her staring at me watching me wondering what the hell I was doing but I didn't let it affect me at all. I didn't miss a beat. I continued packing till all my belongings were in my suitcase without even glancing in her direction and then headed towards the door. It was a horrible thing to do as I look back because I realized that I had manipulated her in the worse way. It was her insecurity from a lifetime of neglect and abandonment and her need for connection, to matter, companionship and to be LOVED that made her fly off of the bed and wrap me up in her arms in desperation.

"WHAT ARE YOU DOING!?" she asked in a high pitch wine.

"You said you aren't going to do what I asked you to do Brooke, that's fine, I ain't going to try to force you to do shit but I ain't just going to sit around here if you ain't even gonna listen to me."

"YOU CAN'T LEAVE!"

"Yea the fuck I can. You ain't even trying to do what I asked you to. We are on 2 different thangs right now. Get off me!" She held tighter.

"Please don't leave Zack. I'll do it…" It was the first time that I noticed the tension in my body. Hearing her finally agree I felt my body relax. I took a deep sigh and I hugged her. I held Brooke, my suitcase right there between the two of us as we embraced.

The rest was history. Between the money she was making, always having ecstasy and bottles of alcohol everywhere and this laid back attitude towards it all I had from my heart not really being in it and having Love for Brooke and so not beating on her and using the scare tactics a lot of other pimps did it wasn't long until her friends saw what was going on and the money being made and joined us. Fresh turnouts became my new drug of choice and I sunk even deeper into objectifying these beautiful woman as I greedily sought to gain more and more money, status and reputation.

Liz...

I saw her post say guys suck and she is over it or something like that. Really all that mattered to me was I saw my way in. Her problems with her boyfriend meant that I could show her some kindness, could speak sweetly to her and tell her I have her back, that she didn't deserve to be with some lame that didn't treat her right or even recognize what he had in his hands and she would swallow it whole. I baited her with my generous flattery and created space for her to be herself and to share in vulnerability. She went for it and my opportunity had come. I sank my fangs into her innocence too deep for her to shake them out of her flesh. After I was confident that I had her in my hands I joked about hoeing and she didn't bat an eye, I told her if she was gonna be fuckin with me we had to be on this paper, she didn't bat an eye. I knew that I had played my cards right and now it would only be a matter of time until she would be making me money. I just needed to coast from here on out. She didn't live in the town so she needed to get up here somehow and I had intended on going and picking her up from the small town she was from just south of Portland but before I could get around to that I was arrested after a show on my birthday. Of course I had drank until I was gurped and popped some Thizz before I went to the venue me and the crew were going to perform at that night. I was higher than a kite by the time it actually came to do our show but I was feeling myself and I was ready. I remember a few of my hitters had come to support the movement so I called them front and center as the beat dropped and I got ready to lace the first song in our set. It was a hella dope track with a funky southern-ish feel but had samples from 'Training Day' on it and had this old school feel too. It was called Desperado and as the bass line filled the room the hook went...

"Dame Pesos/ Me and my desperadoes/ High off the Mota/ Rock yo body with a FO FO/

No time for chavalas/ Nor dem benche levas/ We be stackin' paypa/ Sip Corona on La Playa/"

It was a really funky ass track that had everyone poppin' and swayin'! Watching people dance to your music gives you an amazing feeling! It is god-like to watch your creation move a crowd! It made me feel excited and powerful as I looked down at the audience full of fans enjoying my music.

"Lone star desperado for my fedia/ Bottle to the neck and 2 blunts to the head/ high higher/ you can't get no higher your panocha can get retired/ no 401k/ desperadoes do not pay/ desperadoes do not play/ desperado to my grave/ Stand alone with my back to the wind/ fuck a friend cause no one's there to hold you in the end"

-It was real shit. I prided myself on keepin' all of my words authentic and shit that I had actually done myself I wasn't goin' to be nobodies wanna be studio gangsta I rapped about shit I did and lived my raps sometimes even getting caught up in that, and the ideas cultivated through watching mainstream media and seeing who had money that looked like me that I began feeling as if I HAD to be that shooter or pimp and be hard all the time. On this track though I can hear it and reflect back to how numb I was because it was loneliness I was feelin' clearly but I was so alienated from self that I was just goin to continue livin' this Rock Star lifestyle.-

We was just STARTIN to turn up, the funky bass lines turned to a hyphy bay area style beat! It was ON! The energy was TURNT! I told everyone in the buildin' to get they ass on the dance floor and with that wiped the sweat off my face in that giggin' if ya feel good Bay boy swag and…

" I'm gonna Thizz till I die (die)/ Nigga all I see is pills in my eyes (eyes)/ I know that you like what I converse in my rhymes (rhymes)/ I submerse my whole body up between your bitch thighs (thighs)/ All I take is the finest of these little freak hoes/ I'm armed and ready when I'm off the XO/ Give a bitch no more or less than god damn freak show/ With my 2 fingers down and all the other ones up/ You can find me giggin goin DUMB/ Feelin like the man/ Double fisting the privilege in my hand/ I was on 3 but now I'm on 4/ We all did Molly too man that beezy is a whore/ I'm chilling with a bopper/ linguistics will stop her/ And I'm feelin myself so I'm stewy as I chop her/ Ear/ With irreplaceable game/ I run laps in her brain/ Now she forgetting her lame (lame lame laaaaaaame)...Thizzin outta my body my mind feelin loose/ I done popped about fo' pills and killed an orange juice/ I'm gone of the Henny but really the mini snow bunny wha' hit me/ The Remy too it must have ran up and stuck me/ Thizzin outta my body my mind feelin loose/ I done popped about fo pills and killed an orange juice/ I'm gone of the Henny but really the mini snow bunny wha hit me/ The Remy too it must have ran up and stuck me/ "

The show was by this point at its height and like it I too was high as fuck. I was texting Brooke telling her I wanted some of that birthday sex and she was actin' like she wasn't feelin that. Really she was mad and hurt still because the night before we had drove up to Seattle to cop some bezels and we got into an argument that ended up in us both running out of patience and while driving I mean doing like 80 on the freeway I slapped her and then we started hitting each other while SPEEDING down the I-5 till she pulled over. We had well over 100 years in federal prison sentences worth of illegal shit in the car so after I reminded her of that she got back on the road...

But sitting with that now at 26, remembering watching my mother endure the same violence and thinking about the space I was in at 19 that made it not only ok to jeopardize everyone in the cars life (there was more than me and her) but also that hitting her was the only thing in my mind to try to meet my needs in that moment and that it was ACCEPTABLE. That it had become the norm not just for us in that moment but in our culture and in our society in its entirety to the point where it isn't even surprising, doesn't stir up anger and that rage isn't brought to the surface that specifically domestic violence is taking place saddens me in my heart…

The night of that show, also the night I turned 20 I was arrested for assault, strangulation and harassment. I wasn't in for long but I was in long enough to get really clear on what it was that I wanted to do when I got out. By this time all I wanted to do was live this lifestyle of selling drugs, pimpin' and rappin'. I had popped it with some vets in the game while I was in county and read this book called "Whoreson" by the late great Donald Goines. All I was thinking breathing, eating and shitting was street hustle and how I was going to get further in Life and get as far away from being broke as possible. I was tired of being poor. I wanted to live the American dream. I wanted to have the nice clothes, the cars, the jewelry, vacations and a fat house. And I was so hungry for it at this point that I was willing to do whatever. Even if it meant it had to start with exploiting the 16 year old girl who I had been grooming for the last few weeks to hoe for me.

"Hey what's up baby girl, you good?" I asked Liz

"Oh my god you're out! What the fuck, I missed you!" She exclaimed

"Yea I know I missed you too." I lied. "Look I just got out, I lost everything that I had goin on out here so it is about to be grind time. Its bout to be all work no play till shit get back in place. I don't even have my own spot or nothing right now... I really need your help. If you can come up here and grind with me on some Bonnie and Clyde shit we can probably make it happen. You know me, I am trying to build an empire. You wanna be part of that?"

"Of course I do, you know that I am down for you daddy. I actually came up to Portland looking for you while you were booked but Pedro told me you were in jail and I was hella sad. I am so happy you're out now though. I want to come up there and rock with you."

"A'ight, bet. Do you have any money?"

"Yea I have like $60"

"Okay, buy a bus ticket and come up here ASAP. They are going to be putting me on an ankle monitor until I beat this case so I want you to come up tomorrow baby ok?"

"Wait are you not done with being in jail?"

"No they are letting me out on ankle monitor until my court date. But I am going to beat this case so I ain't even trippin. I just gotta wait till they dismiss it."

"Okay I am going to get on the bus tomorrow then ok?"

"Yup that's perfect. I can't wait to see you!" Honestly it was the money I couldn't wait to see. In those days of incarceration I began to plot out a map getting' gwap so that I could cop all the fly shit I needed to be something and to matter. Not realizing that I already did matter and what would make me the flyest isn't on sale at any store but living right here inside of me. What would make me the dopest was already within me.

When Liz arrived at the Greyhound station I was there to welcome her with a big hug and make her feel welcomed and Loved. I then helped her with her bags and opened her door for her too. We talked for a little while, I went into the specifics of what was going on with me and the courts and what that would mean for how much I could actually be around her. Being that I was going to be getting an ankle bracelet and that it was ordered I be in the house by 9pm I couldn't be out and about rippin' and runnin' the streets. That really made getting' money the way I knew how very difficult so I schooled her on how to sell work too and that it would be most beneficial that as she walked the blade she also sold work. As we drove around the city so I could familiarize her with the different blades in the town I asked her more questions about herself and teased her telling her that I didn't think she had it in her to hoe and that she might not be ready. Of course the playfulness of it was a ploy of manipulation knowing that she would see it as a challenge and want to prove herself to me. It was a sick and twisted game that was being played and could only be played by someone who felt comfortable with the sinister. Someone who felt comfortable in the darkness of evil because an act like this lacked basic empathy and care for another human being, characteristics which are innate amongst all human beings. Well I take that back. I did feel empathy for her, I felt conflicted even about the whole idea of what I was proposing but that same need for more, that desire to have what I did not and the greed I was feeling over rode the empathy and sadness that I was experiencing around having this young woman work for me as a prostitute.

Friday, February 26th, 2010 my case was dismissed. I jumped up when the judge let the words out of her mouth and "My Ambitionz az a Rydah" by Pac came on (at least in my head). "I won't deny it, I'm a straight rydah/ You don't wanna fuck with me/ Got the police bustin' at me/ But they can't do nothing to a G/!" I was feeling ecstatic and bullet-proof! My mom was with me so I started texting the homies and Liz letting them know that I had every intention to get the fuck outta Portland as soon as possible. I decided that I would stay in Portland over the weekend to get tatted up and cop a new phone before I left. The question was where to. I talked to shawty about it, asked her where she wanted to go. We decided on going to either California or Seattle. I decided that I would post an ad for Liz in Cali and in Seattle and wherever the money was would go to next. I posted in Cal first being that it was the beautiful sunshine surfer state and we got a few calls more than usual mostly I am guessing because she was a new face there. After that I posted her in Seattle and soon as I pressed the button to confirm the ad, got damn if the hotline didn't bling! Her phone started ringing off the hook and it was then that I knew we for SURE were headed up to Seattle. Rainy City or not Boeing, Microsoft, Amazon and wherever else these tricks was crawlin' out the wood work from were promising a whole other type of rain. My eyes lit up and that money hungry green guy inside of me started talkin' to me louder than a megaphone in my ear. I was off the ankle bracelet in less than an hour after they dismissed my case and ready to head up to Seattle with the intention of coming back to the Town racked up.

Liz hadn't called me or texted back in over 2 hours. At first I thought maybe I got lucky and she caught a trick on her way back to the hotel but time kept on ticking away and I knew that something wasn't right deep in my gut. I continued to text and call her but there wasn't an answer. Another hour or two went by and I decided that I needed to go to the store she had went to go grab a pick for me thinking that maybe she tried to be slick and steal the pick and that she got caught and was now talking with the security. Also being that she was stopped by the one-time earlier that day my spidey senses were telling me something wasn't right so I left my I.D. at the hotel just in case I got pulled over so I could use my lil brothers name when they ran a check and it come back clean, cause right now, I was technically a fugitive being that I was still on parole back on home turf. And what do you know, as soon as I hit the sidewalk the 50 pushed up on me and started questioning me asking me where I was from and if I knew that there was a big click of surenos not too far from the hotel I was at. He was on me about what I had on, I was wearing yellow and black and had a belt with a 5 pointed star so he kept insisting that I was LK, Latin King. He asked me my name and I told him I was my lil bro, gave him the birthday and everything and he actually let me slide but told me that I needed to be careful. Yeah a'ight is all I thought and kept it pushing towards the Fred Meyers across the street I was hoping to find Liz at. I went in and looked around. Not seeing her I just said fuck it and asked the security if they had dealt with anyone fitting her description. They had not. I got that feeling in my stomach that only a pimp would know as I thought if it was possible that I got knocked for my piece in just that short time from the hotel door to the store. I wasn't sure but I wasn't going to sit around and wait either. I decided that I would go back to the hotel and make a couple more phone calls and if she didn't answer then I would bounce back to the Town. I was concerned for her too it had been a while and already being stopped by the police earlier I had inclination to believe that maybe she got rolled up on again. Earlier that day when she went out to hit the track she was stopped and questioned because she was dressed in a mini skirt and heels so it drew immediate attention to her and the police had questioned her asking her where she was from what she was doing up in Washington and how old she was including who she was here with. She told me after we got back together that she had not told them she was with me but with another woman that she was friends with. I left the store thinking that I would go back to the telly and get my belongings together and then call my home girl to pick me up because shit seemed just plain old fishy. When I walked back into the parking lot of the hotel I saw a white dude in a car that I realized had been there all day. I walked over to the car and saw this muh fucka had a notepad on his lap. When he looked up and saw me looking at him he jumped up startled. I knew then that shit had hit the fan. This was only my second day in Seattle and it started to look like it was taking a turn for the worst. I pushed back towards the back end of the Crossland studio apartment hotel where I had been staying and ducked off into the laundry room. As soon as I got in the door I slid down the wall with my back pressed against it just in time to see the blue and red lights reflected off the ceiling. I got on the phone ASAP and called my home girl and told her I need her to come and pick me up As Soon As Possible! That the police was here. She told me to go to the Fred Meyers across the street and she would swoop me up! I was nervous as shit! Drugs, my suit case and my wallet which had my I.D. were all in the room and if I didn't get them, then it would only be a matter of time until the police put 2 and 2 together and figured out who I was and send a warrant or something to P.O. to come and arrest me. Panicking I decided that I would just try to make a break for it and run across the street to the Fred Meyers where the home girl could come get me. I peeked out the window one last time watching the police bend the block and as soon as I couldn't see his tail lights anymore I ran as fast as I could towards the Fred Meyers! Soon as I hit the corner out of nowhere 2 police gassed up right on top of me and hit the brakes, EEEEEEEERRRK! The two cops hopped out their vehicles guns drawn down on me and yelled for me to get down on the ground. It didn't even occur for me to run, after so many times seeing my mom's boyfriend getting beat down by the police, being assaulted myself and hearing time after time about other black people being shot by these muh fuckas dead in the streets I just stood there frozen in my fear. Eventually my consciousness came back into the reality I was existing in at this moment, I saw the red and blue flashes from the police lights mounted on the car, I heard the whooooooooo of the sirens, I felt the cold night air and light rain on my skin, I saw the two figure with their Glocks drawn, directed and aimed towards my head, I became conscious that the voices I heard screaming "Put your hands up and don't move! If you move I will shoot!" were contradictions coming out of the mouth of these two humans with their guns trained on me. I realized that if they felt at all threatened by my black body the bullets that were in their guns would be in or passing through my body and head, piercing my skin and bone, opening up my body and ripping through my flesh. I surrendered. I got down on the ground. First my knees and then my hands and my knees and then flat. I laid down as the 2 police officers pressed their cold black steel guns into my unarmed body, their knees into my back and gripping my neck shoved my face into the concrete pulling my empty hands behind my back violently shooting pain into my rotator cuff and shoulder. I was caught. Like a wild animal. I was trapped. I had surrendered. I was heading back to the cage. Back to alienation, isolation and dehumanization... I was trapped. I surrendered.

BY NO MEANS have I ever been a stupid individual, in fact growing up they said I was too smart for my own good. But see, being smart is only part of the puzzle, you have to be knowledgeable, wise and understanding too. I definitely lacked the latter two. I think that finally I know what that phrase means now as well. So, if you have ever heard that you are too smart for your own good too and you haven't caught on maybe I can save you some heartache and grief. Being smart, very sharp I thought I could out play everything and everyone, the fact of the matter is there is *ALWAYS* someone maybe not smarter than you but just as smart or a group of people that aren't as smart as you individually but together they got you covered or shit maybe even someone dumb as rocks just been around long enough to have seen your move played before (I hate to break it to you but they say there is nothing new under the sun) and if you're really a bad ass and pass all of those situations, well, then there is a system that ensures if you are smarter and/or more creative than everyone else, especially if you're Black or Brown then you will be made to look criminal (criminalized) or crazy and then be ostracized for being outside the scope of the status quo. This is where Knowledge and Wisdom come into action. Having Knowledge is to KNOW-THE-LEDGE, know YOU and know your limitations. Wisdom is to have a Wise-Dome, or to use your head wisely as in not just think swift and clever thoughts but to think things through and weigh them out. Remember this is Chess and Chess is a Wise man's game, you HAVE to not only think about your move but also how your move will effect the next move, what it will manifest and inevitably craft as the outcome of the Game. Good Chess players see 3-4 moves ahead, but the BEST visualize the end from the beginning.

6 = Equality

Before moving into equality, you have to have equity, equality is to treat everyone the same, that being said if we were to just jump in and start treating everyone the same, the folx who have suffered oppression in this society would still be behind because they are not starting at the same starting point as those that dominant culture supports. Therefore it is mandatory to first build equity before we can access equality, we must not stop at not being sexist, we have to be anti-sexist, we cannot stop at not being racist we must be anti-racist, we must **BE** Nonviolence and anti-oppression and **strive for Pro-Liberation**. However, to access those states first we must become aware, and then we have to find empathy and compassion. Then it is our duty to leverage ANY amount of privilege, agency and status that we have to create space and uplift the voices of the oppressed.

Letter to Liz

Liz,

First and foremost what happened between us is wrong, tragically wrong. I had absolutely no business engaging with you in the way I did let alone at all. That I am behind your experience of prostitution makes me feel guilty and a lot of remorse. It is important for me to tell you that what happened was not your fault. I believe that I manipulated you and used you, abusing your care, support and love towards me. My story is that I saw some vulnerability and took it as an entry point into your life with my intention inevitably you working as a prostitute for me. It's important to me that I tell you, there is nothing wrong with you, you are not a bad person and you did NOT deserve to be treated the way that I treated you. On the contrary, you are smart, witty, brave and full of so much potential. You deserve to be respected, you deserve to be honored, and you deserved honesty and transparency. Maybe most importantly *you deserve freedom and choice.*

I was very manipulative in cultivating our relationship or what I hoped you would perceive as our relationship. I said things that I thought you would want to hear and what I thought would be comforting and boost your confidence. I told myself that this would help me in having my way with you. That you would fall in love with the person or idea of me I was creating and that being in love with that idea of me I would then have control of you. Once I felt I had attained some of that power and control over you I introduced the idea of sex for money I think light heartedly and as a joke.

I see myself as doing this to check how you felt about it without exposing too much of my agenda because I wasn't sure if you would be receptive to the idea yet or not. It troubles and disgusts me now to think when that happened I saw hope that I would get you to work for me. I want you to know that this letter is truly all about empathy for you, me taking responsibility for the damage I believe I did and hope that this has some restorative quality for both of us. That being said I think it would serve both of us to think about the systems we were both oppressed in. I think this is important for you because I am imagining it could be very easy to assume all men or all black men in particular are assholes and out for blood, which I personally do not believe is the case and it is my hope that albeit whatever magnitude of impact I had in your life you learn to not only live with the trauma harmoniously but that you function from your greatness. I believe it's important for you to recognize the institutions and systems too in order to not assume guilt, shame or blame yourself.

I believe you shouldn't take <u>ANY</u> blame for this Liz, none whatsoever.

Another thing I need to clarify is me telling you that I loved you. Although I did grow into caring about you it is important for me to tell you that Loving never looks the way I treated you. To me love is action, and that action is in commitment to the well-being of the person you claim to love. Your well-being was not a priority to me. I was selfish and functioning from a place lacking empathy and compassion for you.

I do not get to tell you how to feel, however I think that anger, that disgust, that being enraged are all valid emotions to feel towards me and the situation that occurred between us. Not only do I think you have the right to be mad I think you should be. I think taking the life from this body that I am in would be justice AND I think you shouldn't let how I treated you lead to any more suffering. I think that finding a space for that anger to exist in a productive way whether it be physical exercise or advocacy, down the line may seem to be beneficial. I'm not completely sure on how to "wrap up" this letter because I have no closure with this myself, I still feel pain, guilt, disgust in myself and shame around the way I saw and acted with you and maybe that will always be there. For now, all I want to get across is that by no means are you to blame for this and I am so sorry that I impacted your life the way I did.

Sincerely,

Zackery Driver

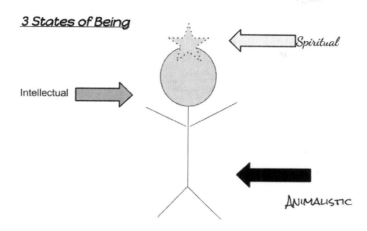

3 States of Being

Spiritual

Intellectual

Animalistic

Others have come before and coined these states the conscious, subconscious and superconscious while others have called them the Id, Ego, and Super Ego. I choose to relate to them simply as the Animalistic State, the Intellectual State and the Spiritual State. I believe that all are constantly engaging and that the diagram that would most accurately represent my thoughts on this matter would be illustrated as 3 constantly shrinking and expanding bubbles. It is my belief that though they are always functioning and sometimes working together one or two of them might hop into the driver seat and expand as the other two or one shrinks to give way to the dominant state of being. For instance, pre-prison I lived my Life in the Animalistic state most constantly and at times when I needed to really strategize or think any clever thought I flowed into my intellectual state or self. And even with the heinous things that I was doing I believe I also continued to maintain even if very discretely a Spiritual State of Being because during my most sinister acts I felt a tug of guilt and sometimes shame. Meaning I had a level of empathy which the Animalistic state is unconscious to and the Intellectual State has no use for although it can intellectualize the concept of the ideas. I believe that we are innately Compassionate, Empathetic and Caring and that those are attributes derived from the essence of our being i.e. one's Spiritual State. I believe that as we think, speak, listen, read, consciously create pattern and habit we enforce our Intellectual State (should not be confused with creating consciousness) and that bubble grows while the Animalistic state shrinks. DO NOT take this the wrong way. The Animalistic state is not "BAD" nor should one try to diminish it or its power. Imagine if you would your child in a burning house, if your Intellect was the only state operating you would calculate and analyze essentially making yourself useless and if it was only your Spiritual state functioning you may say something like "This too shall pass" or "This is only an illusion" resulting in your child burning to death. With the Animalistic state without even understanding or any comprehension at all in the conscious mind we are kicked into gear. This gear is called the Fight or Flight Response (we know now that there are more than just Fight or Flight responses, there is also Freeze, Faun (i.e. Submit) and last but possibly most interesting to me Social Engagement) and it is woven into ALL animals. It is caused by the secretion of chemicals found in our bodies ensuring our ability to save our baby from that burning fire. However that example is not one that we will use on a daily basis unless maybe you are a firefighter so let's look at something more relevant to our day to day Life. Let's look at some of the greatest leaders are world has known whether Malcolm, Garvey, King or even Hitler some of the most powerful animals like lions, bears and bulls have been assigned to these individuals names as attributes of their character. We even say about those who do not give up, are determined and resilient that they have animalistic ambition. For me this points to the validity of my belief that whether engaging the Spiritual or Intellectual state not only holding space for but bringing your animalistic energy with you is a beneficial talent and mandatory for earning yourself a position at the top of the mountain. Before leaving this topic I must explicitly marry the Animalistic state with the Spiritual State. We have a tendency in our dualistic western world to believe that anger, rage yelling or even violence which I attribute mainly to the Animalistic state is a horrible and wrong behavior, that it cannot be Spiritual or come from the Spiritual State. First this is a moralistic judgement and second I do not at all resonate with this. In fact, if we look from the beginning of western religious thought and think about almighty GOD "he" himself delivers violence, Moses killed an Egyptian, Jesus threw the tables and yelled at the merchants in the Temple and if we look at Bhagavad-Gita we see that Arjun on his way to battle his own BROTHER calls out for the Lord he knew as Krishna. Krishna inevitably tells him suck it up and that it is your purpose to be a warrior you must go out and fight your brother and his army! Arjun then ask Krsna to show himself to him and he spontaneously morphs back and forth between what we think of as good and evil as he takes on the body of a loving mother and baby and murderer, two beautiful lovers and a cold rapist, a decrepit old man and an infant full of joy and Life. At seeing this Arjun shrieks and covers his eyes and begs Krsna to stop and then asks what just happened? Krsna answers fundamentally saying that, THIS is what it means to be GOD, to embody ALL aspects, perspectives and experiences of consciousness!

"Strength does not come from physical capacity. It comes from an indomitable will."

-Gandhi

Being as smart as I was soon as I hit mainline it was on, I was going to enroll in every class and every program. I was going to be the star prisoner at least on paper. I figured if I could stack up enough certificates, I could have my way not only in the system with the officials running the show but more importantly once I touched back down in the streets. Even then I had a little bit of wisdom, I knew that if I was going to continue to be in the game I couldn't remain on front street I needed a prop job to at least keep DOC off my back and a little bit of credibility when I got out. For a while I held on to that criminal mindset and how I could get away with instead of do away with that line of thinking. It had a grasp on me! I was literally addicted to the Lifestyle, the power and control that one felt and the thrill and excitement I received being "That Guy". For the invisible man to be seen is a hell of a drug. And for a lot us being the dope boy or pimp was the most accessible way we could meet that need. Eventually the grip of the street grew weak enough for me to escape it as my knowledge expanded and my spirit grew. But it definitely wasn't overnight, it was a process that took deconstructing and healing my mind and spirit and Truth be told I continue to struggle with the residue of that Life on my spirit and psyche today. Knowing me you know I had million dollar schemes brewing in my mind and so opening up my own business was going to be MANDATORY! I needed to not only MAKE money but also to launder the money I was planning on making behind the scenes in the street (yup, I had smarts, even a little Wisdom but I lacked Understanding). It was with these thoughts that I began learning carpentry skills like Drywall, roofing and siding and enrolled with the homebuilders association. I studied Accounting and Business and earned a degree in Small Business Management through Clark College. I also went for Graphic Design and got involved with Toastmasters all of these played a part in developing my mind but I believe that it was the BOOKS that I READ that really brought me the most intellectual development. I began reading books for entertainment, I read what we would call "Hood Books" at first, books about brothers that were making their way in the game in fictionally big moves, like running across some jake and robbing them for a hundred birds and then creating his own Mafia. Haha yeah it was super science fiction some of the stuff even one story was told of some drug dealer going into enemy territory and giving everyone Tims that had C4 inside of them and then after he had passed them all out and put some space between him and the unfortunate gangstas he pushed the transmitter and blew off their feet! It was definitely entertaining work at first, but as my mind shed the haze of drugs and alcohol and began to enjoy the solitude and spaciousness I found being imprisoned, those books began to lose their sparkle and contrary to popular belief it was only the young or immature men inside of the prison system that filled their time reading these books. Most read books like Art of War by Sun Tsu or 48 Laws of Power by Robert Green and if they were reading fiction books it was the books that were about castles and dragons and those thankfully never caught my attention. So, with my desire to learn, grow and make myself as powerful an individual as I possibly could I picked up my first book outside of the foolish entertainment. Letter to a Young Brother: Manifest Your Destiny by Hill Harper It was a book that essentially was a black man writing letters to younger black men. For me it was the first time I experienced a successful, educated and pro-social black male, period. And as I read through its pages it literally revolutionized my mind on the possibilities of what a respectable black male could be or is.

I AM A BLACK BEING

I am not Snoop Dogg or 50 cents depiction of youth caught in the trap of poverty

I AM A BLACK MAN

I am not a celebrity actor nor sports phenom

I AM A BLACK WOMAN

I am not a gang banger nor do I sell drugs to your children

I AM A BLACK MAN

I am not here for your sexual objectification

I AM A BLACK WOMAN

I am not a thief to be followed through your grocery store

I AM A BLACK MAN

I am not contagious my skin isn't a disease there's no need to cross the streets when you see me coming

I AM A BLACK WOMAN

Media portrays me to be criminal and dangerous but

I AM A BLACK MAN

And with this evil portrayal made to look glamorous and cool

I begin to produce stress in my mind

With the cognitive dissonance that then comes alive

When I want to be good but that's contrary to the media's hype

So

In this situation I have two options from which I can decide

Anti-social or prosocial release of this blockage in my mind

I can pick up a book educate myself and fight,

Seldom earning temporary status in the upstream struggle of rank established by the invention of white,

Colonization, domination, capitalism and privilege handed to those who are "Right"

But then I am ambushed from both my left and my right

My people barely except me because I no longer fall into the culture and identity created by MTV, BET ESPN

So I'm left to stand damn near by myself against white privilege

My friends and family asking me why I sound so white

And them too feeling ostracized because my linguistic capability high

So then it's me against the world as I face odd looks as I walk into this white space to purchase clothing for my interview

Walk up to the counter and now I'm either a ball player or a rapper

I'm also not the 15 minutes early I planned to be to this racist institution

Because I was pulled over by an officer who wanted to turn me back into a slave legally based off the 13th amendment of the constitution

I AM A BLACK MAN

(In the first section of the 13th Amendment of the Constitution of the United States it states that: "Neither slavery nor involuntary servitude, except as a punishment for crime whereof the party shall have been duly convicted, shall exist within the United States, nor any place subject to their jurisdiction." The Thirteenth Amendment to the United States Constitution abolished slavery and involuntary servitude, EXCEPT as punishment for a crime. Shit it was/is a "CRIME" to be BLACK! It was a LOOPHOLE to getting rid of slavery as they knew it then and still holding a legal way to maintain ownership of slaves. And we all know that the rich Love their loopholes. WAKE UP!)

As my mind grew stronger and my spirit lighter I didn't find the books that I used to read interesting any more, I began to hunger for learning, after so many years of not being given the true Living water, I was thirsty! My book shelf went from shoot 'em up bang bang, lets sell all the drugs to books on business's organizational culture and real estate from there it transformed again to philosophy and spirituality.

I began to become conscious of my breathing.

Whether lying or sitting or even in sport I would think about the breath I was taking, intentionally fill my stomach with oxygen instead of just my upper chest as they would call it, expanding or breathing from my diaphragm. I did this because the benefits were obvious once I took a second to think about it… I could go without food for weeks and my body survive, even thrive for a while, I could go without water for days but I could only go without oxygen, the air I breathe 24/7 for a matter of minutes before I would pass out or die. I thought about how when you become excited or happy you take a DEEP breath in and your eyes expand but when you're scared or angry your body and breaths are tight and short so it made sense for me to breathe deeply and fully and as I read more especially books that exhibited Eastern philosophy I gained more understanding of how are breath is equal even to our energy and how we function. All of which made sense when I just took a second to think about it. I remember the first time I was reading a book and thinking about my breath, or breath consciousness dawned on me and I smiled because I knew that it was a gift to remember to breathe and how blessed it was to feel my breath travel past my nostrils and through my throat and opening my belly, the relaxation it created. It was a gift that not even prison could take from me after it had stripped me naked. And it was a gift I could continuously give to myself and share with those I Love! I guess it was the first lesson of Self Love. From thinking about my breath as I breathed I began to train my mind to allow more Knowledge and Creativity inside of it by imagining the possibility of being able to see out of my forehead or open up my mind. I would imagine being able to see into the planetary system, into the galaxy and then into the Universe. Yet I would also train myself to feel solid and grounded by doing the reverse and imaging the possibility that my body was like a mighty oak tree and that as I breathed in I took up all of the energy and richness of Earth and as I exhaled roots from my feet grew down into the earth first deep and then wide. In this way I was connected to the Heavens and I too was connected to the Earth. This allowed me to stay focused, to contemplate and to think critically and it was in those places while I read books like The Four Agreements by Don Miguel Ruiz, Healing The Child Within by Charles L. Whitfield and Tuesdays with Morrie by Mitch Albom that I had epiphanies and realizations. I began to break out of the mold I was placed into when they told me I was black so I had to act like be like talk like (_____). It was with Napoleon Hill's 'Think and Grow Rich A Black Choice' that it really solidified itself in my mind that I HAD to GUARD my mind because there was actually an attack on it or fight for what would consume it and that I needed to be careful what I spent my time doing. Islam was greatly valuable during this time too because of the structure and discipline for one but also some of the Hadith (i.e. the stories that the Prophet would tell or things he would be seen doing) were those of being vigilant because the Jinn and Shaytan were always looking for a way in, would even crawl into your booty if you laid on your stomach to sleep. Don't get me wrong I would watch a movie or listen to some shoot 'em up bang bang shake your ass music but the difference was I KNEW it was entertainment now, I didn't live my life having to personally identify with murder and selling drugs. It was a Life I lived but it wouldn't be a choice for my Life again. And actually there was a while that I didn't even watch the tube. It was nothing more than a dust collector. Just take a second and think about it... Television... TELL A VISION and what are shows called? Programs or if you remember when there was an emergency announcement... "Please forgive us for interrupting your REGULAR PROGRAMMING" the shit is right there under your nose, the signs surround us... Television, TELLS US A VISION AND PROGRAMS OUR MIND! Let that be an invitation to turn off the damn housewives of Atlanta, love and hip hop or whatever other "REALITY" t.v. programs there are right now and pick up a fuckin book!) There is nothing there to support us at all, it is all drama or plain trifling. Even in school when we open up our textbook it is as slaves and peasants that we are represented, when we watch a movie we are portrayed to either be super celebrities or petty criminals and our legacy, OUR LEGACY! Is NEVER told! There is no mentions of how our philosophy and technology was secretly swindled out of Africa by Europeans and then translated into Greek to create the cultural appropriation they then sold as their own, how our people were kidnapped and stolen, there is no mention of how it is a fact that our culture and people were the epicenter for intellectual GENIUS and RADICAL spiritual development! Even today we can ask someone to explain the socioeconomic status of Africa and they will probably imagine a potbellied anorexic child hiding in a bush while yet in reality there are SKYSCRAPERS and pristine beaches ALL throughout our beautiful homeland. Not to mention pyramids and other structures that today thousands of years later are yet to be explained by modern day science. Gold, diamonds, oils, and other precious commodities exported from Africa at such a rate that they are trading for over $100billion in any given moment. Not a million but a BILLION! Just in exports! And muh fuckas running around talkin about they ballin' when they touch a 100k!? In fact Africa's GDP Growth has outperformed the USA and the rest of the WORLD with faithful victories since at least 2010! But these are things that are not talked about let alone taught to us as students while we are in our crucial developmental years forming the way we will identify in the world. I would even go a step further to say they are HIDDEN. This Knowledge is intentionally withheld while the portrayal of a poor and humiliating Africa is made prevalent so that we grow up with an inherent illusion of having no value or worth within ourselves and/or our culture and what is taught then, is that in order to be cool, in order to be powerful, and in order to be successful we must attain things, whether that means competing against each other, whether it mean poisoning and/or killing each other, stepping on one another or becoming just as savage as the oppressor and falling in suit with the mindset of capitalism. WAKE UP! We have to use OUR head we have to think with OUR OWN HEAD instead of passively accepting what is handed to us! If you really want to get on some paper put the guns and dope down and pick up some Kemtic Philosophy books, Napoleon Hill, or The Secret by Rhonda Byrne and learn about the Universal Law of Attraction that INSISTS the Universe MUST GIVE YOU what you dwell upon!

It was with these thoughts swirling around in my mind that I knew I needed to get real clear on what I wanted in Life and what I held dear. I took a really deep look within myself and asked what is it that I value in Life? First I thought shit, Money. But I had learned by this time to always ask Why. So I asked myself WHY money? Because I don't want to be broke, I heard myself say. But, why don't you wanna be "broke"? Because I want to buy things. Why do you wanna buy things? Because you have to have things. Why do you have to have things? Well you have to have a car and a house and clothes... So as I pruned this idea that I had to have money down it became obvious to me that it wasn't Money that I valued it was the options and choice that that strategy gave me, the Autonomy or in other words Freedom it provided. I valued Freedom, but Money wasn't a value it was a strategy to get my need for Freedom/Autonomy met! Realizing this was so freeing I mean imagine if money was what you valued and you were in prison making at the most 35 cents an hour! It would be HELL! But what I did was asked myself Why till I got to the CORE of what it was I truly

NEEDED or valued when I said that I valued money. I also realized through this line of processing besides Freedom I also wanted money to buy things because lacking Knowledge of Self and Spiritual Realization internally I was starving to be seen and I was still under the illusion that material wealth would fix that being broke internally and longing for Self-Love, Security and Stability. I realized that I really valued Family, Connection, Love, Acceptance, Affection and Belonging. Realizing all of these things I eventually wrote down what it was that I valued and I put them in numeric order from what I valued the most down. Sure enough Autonomy/Freedom was on the very top followed by Belonging, Affection and Love. Later I came to understand that Trust and Authenticity were big values for me as well! Reflecting back, it is very interesting to play with the idea of whether we hold these values dear because we practice them every day and do not know what we would do without them or if it is because we lack them and therefore have a deep need for them to find some form of balance and equanimity in our lives. What really put things into perspective for me around this concept however, was when I read about Maslow's Hierarchy of needs and the psychology around human needs. I found that EVERYthing we do is based off of a need being or not being met. EVERYTHING! So to be conscious of your needs is a must in order to transcend.

There was no more time for playing cards and slappin' bones because my needs had changed. My need for play which was coupled with a need for ease and peace of mind, maybe even harmony due to the isolation and loneliness I was feeling being in prison after I found myself aware of them spontaneously shifted to needing to learn, grow, and create independence and Freedom for myself. So, I got deeper into my studies every day. One book after another, quote by quote breaking down the barriers and expanding my mind. One tape after the next. Everyday became a study day for me. I would workout, read books, watch religious and financial tapes, talk on the phone and eat. I remember one day a partner of mine had come up to me and said "Ay yo D man, I been watchin' this dude and he stays going over to the phone with a paper with a ton of letters and numbers on it. It looks like he is runnin stocks." "Oh for real?" "Yeah man, I am gonna push up on him and ask him about it but I was thinking though that we could invest money with him. If you still wanted to find a way to flip some doe maybe he could help you." Sure enough, later that day we were back on the unit and my partner Charles pointed this guy out to me. I walked over by him and looked at his paper. I saw numbers under letters. LOTS OF THEM! It was actually very exciting to me because I had remembered watching this movie when I was a kid about a big shot stockbroker and I had always thought the profession would be exciting and challenging. As soon as the guy hopped off the phone Charles went and asked him what was up and then called me over and introduced us. G, as he asked to be called was definitely right there from within the prison making moves in the stock market! I wanted to know ALL about it! I asked him if he would mentor me in it and he said yes. From then forward I was watching CNBC like the channel was going to die within the next couple days from terminal illness and I was taking notes like a madman. Jim Cramer became my hero and favorite friend. I started reading everything I could get my hands on that dealt with the market. Very quickly those letters and numbers began to mean something to me and as my understanding the power of the stock market and also real estate grew, understanding how powerful of a tool they are my frustration and anger towards my family did so as well. I was pissed off that I had not had the privilege to have been told about these financial tools long ago! WHY WAS IT I WAS JUST NOW LEARNING ABOUT THESE THINGS!? It made no sense to me that they would keep this away from me! I had not yet put any real money into the Market but with what I was calculating and estimating I was right on point every time except for once and even that loss wasn't bad! So as I sat in prison for trying to make money the wrong way I grew pissed the fuck off that access to this other way was withheld from me and I was seeing MILLIONS of dollars being traded on it every damn day. Day in and day out faithfully. This was really where it was at! These humans were making millions of dollars a day some of them without even leaving their own homes! Or by touching a few buttons on their iPhones while they were far away from their homes out on a beautiful beach! It was completely mind blowing! I eventually called my people and had them put the little bit of money I had floating around in the free world in a stock account and I would call my moms and she would maneuver the funds as I requested the best she could sometimes resulting in frustration but she had my back though and guess what… Lil homie from the hood that wasn't even allowed to go to regular class because he had "special needs" actually STRUCK and I too made some paper in the stock market without a computer, without spreadsheets and market analysis tools just hard work in my studies, diligent vigilance, listening and intuition. That latter one, by all the big wigs was a skill frowned against. For me though I began to rely on my intuition and it turned out to be fruitful! In a matter of a quick couple months I turned my $500 into just below $1,400 and although I laugh at myself now that shit was stressful then even though it was just pocket change to most folks in the market.

Money's cool, don't get it twisted you will never hear me say money is the root of all evil. I am not confused I know that money isn't the root of evil but that it is CAPITALISM which is. Yet, we cannot be strictly about business 24/7 that wouldn't be a holistic approach to Life and we are a holistic and multi-dimensional being. We have to get in touch with our deeper side. Take time throughout our day for understanding. It is also important to Know where you come from. Most of our people do not know where they come from but thankfully Knowledge has been dispersed so it doesn't matter how far you may find yourself from Africa now because Africa is never far from YOU. What do I mean by that I am sure you are asking… Well think about it… Ancient Kemetic Proverb (Yes Kemet, I call that land that society would like to label Egypt by its African name which is Kemet. The name Egypt only came along after white people came through the land, pillaged it and colonized it giving the Holy City the exonym it is currently being identified with) say: "As Above So Below" … Look at the beautiful spiral on your finger, the spiral then of the nautilus shell all the way at the bottom of the sea then expand your vision to encompass the infinite beauty of the spiral we know as the Milky Way Galaxy. Have you heard of Phi? Phi in Greek is the 21st letter (oh how the great archer smiles) and to the artist of the Renaissance the Divine Proportion. It is the solution to an equation. Phi constructs the Solar System and Universe, it is the distances between planets, the structure of Saturn's rings, and it gives shape to the formless. "As Above, So Below"... It exist in the arrangement of molecules and the core of quantum matter and time. It points to Truth, the truth of the Supreme Mathematics and the Supreme Mathematics points to Love, Righteousness and Truth on our path…

"When you are inspired by some great purpose, some extraordinary project, all of your thoughts break their bonds. Your mind transcends limitations; your consciousness expands in every direction; and you find yourself in a new, great and wonderful world. Dormant forces, faculties and talents become alive and you discover yourself to be a greater person than you ever dreamed yourself to be."

-Patañjali

The Supreme Mathematics

1. Sun; Knowledge; Man

2. Moon; Wisdom; Woman

3. Stars; Understanding; Children

4. Culture/Freedom

5. Power/Refinement

6. Equality

7. Divine Being –Goddess/God

8. Build Positivity and Destroy Negativity

9. Born

0. Cypher

I had found the teaching of Clarence 13X right on time as the Universe always provides what you need when you are READY and right when you need it. Seekers of Truth never harbor and act stingy with Knowledge that they are blessed to gain so as soon as it was possible another God handed me this book by Dr. Supreme Understanding Allah and some other members of the Nation of Gods and Earths and I immediately dove into it head first! A beautiful thing happens with my being when I read a book that actually grabs my attention and propels me to read it. I literally get sucked into the pages of the book. If I am reading a Buddhist book well then I embody the mind of Siddhartha and my Life is committed to his teachings even gets into his knowingness as I empty myself to give space to the words I find there. If I read about Huey P. Newton and the Black Panther Party for Self Defense then I take on the attitude, militancy and strength of the Vanguard and make it my mission to demand the 10. So when I picked up this book 'Knowledge of Self' I was ALL about man being the Supreme Being and only answering to the Supreme Mathematics that was also me and governed the Universe. I memorized the Math instantly (I later came to know that this ability to download information was what some would call being in Integration Mode). And my family and friends learning this Knowledge was my number one priority! I called my partner and went over the Math until she had memorized it and once she had I would quiz her on it to make sure that she had it down. When we would talk we would ask each other what was the Math of the day. For example, Today is March 17th, so the math would be for the

17th in this situation. 1=Knowledge and 7=GOD and then you also add those numbers together which would create 8. 8= Build Positivity Destroy Negativity. So if someone asked what's the Math of the Day the answer would be... "Knowledge God all being Born into Build and Destroy". If you were really poppin it the conversation wouldn't end there, you would elaborate on it. Because it is a Universal Truth the numbers and their meaning stay the same but the story we tell will always be different because we experience different perspectives of reality. For instance, when Astrid asked me how I saw the Math today I said "Knowledge God all being Born into Build and Destroy... Writing this book my goal is to spread Knowledge of the Divine being inside of us all and having that Knowledge of God bears the righteous ability to Build Positivity and Destroy Negativity." Sometimes the Mathematics may be very deep and sophisticated for you and other times it may be that Man Woman all being Born into Children, or another way to say that is that Knowledge and Wisdom Bear Understanding. This is the Supreme Mathematics.

The other teaching I soaked in was a teaching that Allah - The only thing worthy to be praised and worshipped, the Supreme Being- was actually closer to us than we had realized. The teaching was that WE are the ALLLAH, or Only thing worthy to be worshipped and frankly it made a lot of sense. After Nature or the Supreme Mathematics we dominate and govern the Earth. This just is, and it puts us on the height of the food chain which in this context means that we are Supreme Beings. If not as a spiritual practice it definitely was empowering for someone who had been oppressed and underprivileged their entire existence to grasp this concept. It was one of the times I was able to flirt with the idea that we are all divine and that there is more to our being than what meets the eye, something is there that points to an Interdependence.

For the longest time I was trying to track down this book by Robert Green. Everyone I came across I asked for the book and it was either being read or checked out already. For years even now I hear so much about it, that it was a MUST read and would teach me the secrets of creating power and how to utilize it over other people, but when I finally did get my hands on it, I couldn't read through the 48 Laws of Power... As I began to read the book I experienced this heavy sensation and the vibe of the book which was full of lies, deceit and manipulation just didn't jive with my own personal vibe so I pushed myself to read a little bit more but inevitably I had to put the book down before getting even half way through it. I just was no longer interested in that diabolical power and control. I had come to a place in my Life where that manipulation was just no longer Life giving. I was much more connected to Love. Too connected with the humanity of other people to get inside of this book that was created based on oppressing other beings.

"When the Power of Love overcomes the Love of Power the WORLD will know Peace."

Jimi Hendrix

As I began to clear my head of all of the garbage and toxicity that had been injected into my thoughts so deeply that it became woven into who I am it was obligatory for me that I begin filling the space with positive, productive and prosocial things. The brain unless you are like a super nun or monk will ALWAYS wander to find a place to dwell and as we think so we shall become and attain. So I began to study Yoga one of the first books I read was called Yoga Youth and Reincarnation by Jess Stearn. Read it! As I began to read books about Yoga and start my own Yoga practice one of the things that dawned on me was that we are ALL doing Yoga… Maybe even all the time!

Because it comes from a different culture and religion and because when we see it over here we see a bunch of skinny white woman in lulu lemon spandex eating tofu on kale chips the meaning and beauty is lost. Yoga is a Sanskrit word meaning Union. There are 8 different branches of Yoga that we can or are practicing. Karma Yoga (selfless action), Siddha Yoga (chanting) and Raja or Royal Yoga (controlling your mind, body and emotions) just to name a few. The limb or path of yoga that has the most visibility here in the States is Hatha Yoga which is Yoga involving movement and breath. Patanjali who has been coined the "Father of Yoga" wrote a Sutra (book) called the Yoga Sutra and this practice of Hatha draws from the teachings in that Sutra a lot. There are 3 main parts to this Yoga. First is Pranayama which is your breath and vitality. The most important is to breathe. Second is Dhrishti which is focus but more than focus, it is a laser like focus. If focusing is what you did when you were thinking about hitting a nail with a hammer, Dhrishti would be compared to becoming so focused on the hammer and the nail that you actually become the hammer and the nail, no way you're going to hit your thumb then! This helps you to see the world as it really is. The third piece is the Asana or the postures. The health benefits from this Yoga alone are tremendous and have been proven! The piece until recently I was discounting was the emotional and spiritual effect. But after an experience that I just encountered I know personally that the emotional and spiritual aspects of our being are effected through the movement of our body as well. One reason being that we hold trauma somatically. I am specifically recalling the first time that I let go and got really deep into my half pigeon which is a yoga asana that stretches the hips and glute muscles on either side of your body when you practice it. Before the time in particular I had of course done this asana but I never went very deep because it was an uncomfortable pose. Well, this time I was in the middle of a 40 Day yoga challenge where we were challenged to do yoga 6 days a week for 40 days, to push our bodies and expand our minds in hopes of breaking through old barriers and limiting beliefs and reaching new heights. All that being said when it came time to perform half pigeon I did my normal only gently touching the discomfort of this pose and then I thought to myself *you're in the midst of this 40 day challenge Zack, push past your old limits and break through your barriers.* With that, I let go and pressed my chest and forehead down to the mat, I felt my hips and ass muscles stretch and I began to cry as an overwhelming wave of deep sadness and grief washed over my entire body, I just stayed in the pose for what seemed like forever, crying, sobbing, experiencing the emotion that rolled over and through my body and mind. I realized that yes it was uncomfortable to get into that posture but that wasn't why I was not allowing myself to get into that pose because there were several that were uncomfortable. I learned that day that the being was subconsciously pushing me away from that pose because I was still holding trauma there from when I was sexually abused and further more I believe the suppression of my sexuality via my religious upbringing resided there as well and this posture when fully expressed unlocked it and released the pain and sadness that was held there. Yoga also gave me more grounding and slowly began to open me up. When I did my first inversion and took a shoulder stand with my feet up in the air where my head normally is and felt all of the blood rushing back to my heart and head it was amazing. It gave me a definite rush and charged me energetically.

5 Pointed Star Philosophy for Growth, Development and Cultivation

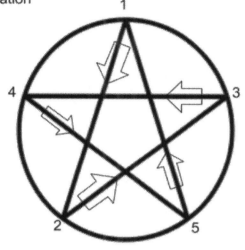

1. Knowledge.
2. Truth.
3. Righteousness.
4. Love.
5. Loyalty.

If you take one look at my body you will see that I have an obsession with stars. At this current moment I already have 11 stars tattooed on my body. A real star is a violent combustion of gasses burning so hot that they shine bright enough to bring Light millions of miles away to Earth, to other planets and throughout the galaxy. Several times I have heard other people being called stars. I myself have been called a star and I have heard people talk about a radiance I exude. I began to think of stars in the more tangible stylized representation like what is above and asked myself Why was it that people said I was a star? What makes one shine in the community? I thought about what it was people really valued about me that made them place value on my presence in their Life and I asked myself what did I find worthy, what did I exhibit? Having the obsession I did with stars I started playing with different words at the points of the star. I didn't start with all of the same ones that are there now and it was a while tell they took the exact order that they are in but eventually after a lot of mulling over, contemplation and refinement my philosophy on Growth, Development and Cultivation came into fruition and it related directly to the object of my obsession and explained to me why those who follow this path shine, synchronicity.

First is Knowledge, ALWAYS. SEEK Knowledge and with Knowledge comes the ability to perceive Truth. Truth is the second step and it is in Understanding the Truth that you can then act and that action is Righteousness. Righteousness is the 3rd step, when you act FROM the Truth there is only one thing that can come from that and that is Righteousness and being a Righteous being living in tune with your own spirit and consciousness we begin to not only Love ourselves and others but others begin to Love us. When one is fully in their integrity and alignment with Self it is the natural order that these feelings rise up in others when the presence of our being interacts with them authentically (think of Nelson Mandela and the prison guards who would fall in love with him and have to be replaced on a regular basis). This is the power of Love and Love is the 4th aspect of the Star. The 5th aspect of the Star is Loyalty. As that connection with Self begins to strengthen as your Love grows not just for others but for yourself it cultivates a Loyalty to your conscious, to your spirit and to your vision and goals. As people watch you do you, it also cultivates Loyalty for inside of your community and creates the space you need to be Loyal to the needs of the community as well. Even the Earth in whole which you currently Live and share with all beings before and after you. Full Circle that Loyalty also brings you back to Seeking Knowledge because Knowledge, Wisdom and Understanding are the steps to Enlightenment and Liberation. And it is True we cannot pour from an empty cup. As we enter into the world and share what we have been blessed with we MUST also utilize self-care taking care of ourselves with relaxation, fitness, vacation and most importantly continue to stretch ourselves as we learn and grow. If you are not moving forward you are going backwards. There is no contentment in standstill, only stagnation. And procrastination is the poison of our dreams so it is required we move towards progress.

Even if the movement is moving deeper within your own self still we must move. In fact in terms of Liberation the most important movement isn't visible when tracking for external actions it is only known by the knower and those knowing because it is an internal process in which we find True Freedom, Prosperity and Greatness Beyond Measure.

Muhammed said on Jihad, that Jihad of the physical being, fighting and war was the lesser of Jihad, and not necessarily desired, but that Jihad Al Nafs, or the Struggle/Fight of The Spirit or Consciousness was the MOST important battle that we can ever fight. Deconstructing the false self and getting back in alignment with the natural order of things, in tune with Universal Love, this is the calling.

And with that I would spend hours in the library, I began to seek Knowledge ALL the time. Reading and talking with people, to LEARN became my obsession. 24/7 I wanted to learn and grow. It brought me across some really interesting stories and material such as Behold a Pale Horse by Milton William Cooper and Zachariah Sitchin's Genesis Revisited. I began to read literature published by extremely alternative schools of thought compared to what I was used to. I read about things like how the Earth was created and even how we human beings had come into existence. I read about our own electromagnetism and the electric meridian lines of the Earth even some authors stating that Stonehenge and other epic configurations could have very well been placed there with an intent and purpose to sabotage the path of these meridian lines throwing the Earth off kilter. I read about FBI and CIA specifically CO-INTEL PRO sabotaging and assassinating powerful members of the Black Nation that were promising Liberation for the oppressed and how they targeted organizations that had the grassroots power of their community backing them up as they stood in defense of the exploitation of their people. C.R.I.P. for one. If we just listen to what media and police say then we think that this is a malicious group of people that was founded to wreak havoc on the community, sell drugs and rob folks. The Truth is that C.R.I.P. stood for C.ommunity or C.alifornia R.evolution I.n P.rogress and that it was started to protect the vulnerable people in the black community against whiteness, police brutality to name one act of whiteness specifically. The government said to themselves "oh, well hell no we cannot have that" and designed plans to take out the most authoritative individuals, bring in drugs that they themselves went to Asia and South America to get and created in laboratories. Who they couldn't bribe they would incarcerate and who they couldn't incarcerate they would kill. This was mandatory for the large home with the white picket fence 2.5 kids and a dog/cat to exist. The American dream could not exist without the exploitation of the underprivileged and that population after the horror of slavery consisted of a majority of melanated people or in other words black and brown bodies. People of Color. The dismantling and corruption of C.R.I.P. was not the only time that this took place. In fact the ONLY time in the HISTORY of the United States of America where we orchestrated our OWN military to perform an airstrike on our OWN domestic soil was the black holocaust during the destruction of Black Wall Street. After slavery had been "abolished" Black woman and men came together and created what was called Black Wall Street. It consisted of 600 business, 21 churches, 30 grocery stores, 2 movie theatres, 6 airlines, 1 hospital, 1 bank and its own school system!

143

This once again threatened the comfortability, power structure and profitability of capitalism for those who are white. Thus from the perspective of "We The People" or let me spell it out here... white heterosexual cisgender able bodied Anglo-Saxon Christian men this beautiful monolithic community needed to be destroyed. These two points of history that I mention are by far not the only ones in the history of systemic oppression where genocide, manipulation and lies were being used to uphold the status quo here in the United States and there are things yesterday and today that continue to go on that are very subtle and covert such as school-to-prison pipeline, gentrification and redlining, miseducation, socialization through media, the drug war and all the implicit and not so implicit bias all of these different cogs in the machine create to result in black and brown bodies being frisked and shot down in the streets by the police even if they are only 5 years old or 85 years old today at rates that are exponential when compared to white folks. I wouldn't be inside my integrity if I didn't at least mention the HORROR that First Nation peoples, folx who are indigenous to this land experienced as colonizers came to their home and began these brutal acts. My Native American siblings are in large left out of the stories of oppression and their pain not heard while the focus has been on Black, LGBTQ or Class issues, however this land that we are 24/7 standing on was stolen from them, their ancestors murdered savagely, at times being hung over fire and burned alive. This is hitting black and brown people the hardest but it isn't just a phenotypical issue. The Georgia stones point us in the direction that we are heading towards given the authority of the current power brokers of this world. They state to "Maintain humanity under 500,000,000 people in perpetual balance with nature". The most current world population I've seen says that there are 7.125 BILLION people on this Earth. How many people then does that mean have to die so that this is possible? This is population control and who will feel this the most are those of us who because of the beneficiaries of systemic oppression greed and need for more are now underprivileged. This is already happening around us when an invisible war is being fought whether for nuclear bombs a country doesn't even possess or as you reach for the gun that was really just your cell phone. War is being waged on humanity and it's in the food, it is in the media it is even in our own mind full of the programming that the elite have designed for us to receive.

What Are They Afraid Of

What are they afraid of

I'll tell you what they are afraid of

They are afraid of 1 million black fist

Raised high as we march through the Capitol

1 million black men coming together on some tactical

Organization

To save our Beautiful Black Nation

Knowledge of Self

The Key to Salvation!

Algorithms of the Supreme Mathematics vibrate
through my mind

Intune with the sun and the moon standing divine

Cultivating Inner Peace

As I elevate Kundalini through my spine

3rd Eye illuminating the darkness (as I enter the light)

Bringing forth understanding lost upon the Blind

Seeing Religion, mainstream media, poverty,
systemic education and prison all intertwined

Violent inhalation because I can't believe my own
mind

No honestly I can't believe my own mind...

AKA a computer program downloading regurgitated tradition passed down through the lies

From those suffering the corruption of the greedy generations who have raped and pillaged throughout time

Articulating what I crave to be an original thought

But the neurons all fire inside a brain that had been robbed, stolen and bought

The plot

Is deeper than it seems to be

Our identity

Passed through more hands than a centipede

Google straw man, Rosicrucian, epic of Gilgamesh

Babylonia, Sumer and Ancient Kemet

Mesopotamia

The theory of Annunaki

Then David Icke

To open up your psyche

Don't be surprised if you see me on the nightly

Victim of "gang violence" cause truth in the media is highly unlikely

You saw what happened to Pac when he started talkin about whitey

After this drop the whole 10% gonna want more than fight me

But BITE ME

And if you can't see it by now

Then shit I ain't for the circus I can't fuck with you clowns!

"I freed a thousand slaves

I could have freed a thousand more

if only they knew they were slaves."

-Harriet Tubman

Letter to My Mother

Mama,

I am less than 175 hours from being released from prison once again, however, now for the last time. I will never see the insides of her belly again. It brings me delight, yet there is a soft sweet sorrow, for over the many years I have spent within her she has forced me to Love and Appreciate her. If not for the solitude she provides me with then most definitely for the challenge to grow from boy to man. If not for her many libraries and educational programs, well, then for the space and time she affords me to strengthen my body, mind and spirit... She has transformed me. She is the chrysalis in which I have undergone my metamorphosis from extortionist of my own Beauty and soul to the Monarch who enjoys the symmetry of Love, Peace, Joy and Harmony coupled with Ambition, determination, discipline and the need for excellency. The Monarch who is now amused by the idea of an impossible task. She has developed an animalistic ambition inside of me.

The fervent desire to Live of those who exist inside her cold embrace without hope of seeing the free world lives inside of me! It creates synergistic passion to attain and achieve every Dream and Aspiration that burns hotter than 10 million Suns. I AM the SUN, in an eternal state of Super-Nova, which is why I SHINE, and those who see me speak of my glow. I am A Son. Rejected by his father, betrayed by his mother, disowned by his grandfather, yet I AM A SON! Son of my strong and immoveable concrete mama, the only one who whether I was good or bad, whether I yelled and cursed her or spoke words of adoration in a sweet deep tone, she held me, she clothed me, she fed me when I was hungry. Her nurturing was unconditional. It was only I, in a state of youthful ignorance who forced her hand into discipline and rejected her jewels.

I am a man now, and with less than 175 hours until I am released from her embrace I feel as if I am spending the last of a few moments with my longest and dearest Lover. The most Committed and Understanding Lover I have ever had. However heart aching it is to leave her comfort, still I must go. Her promise still rings in my ear, she has made an undying promise that if ever I should turn back, her bed will be waiting and her passion will be hot. But even in the midst of her lust she whispers, "I Believe in YOU", and she reminds me of every lesson we have learned together. She becomes my friend and encourages me to leave her and let her go, she becomes a martyr as she invites my release because she knows that with every step my feet take towards my inevitable success, she becomes a fond yet distant memory. Nonetheless, the precious jewels she entrusted me with from her very own dowry continue to shine as I convey her message and lessons as we agreed upon before she endowed me with her beautiful treasure. Her message is painful today but it brings hope for tomorrow, she enjoys the company of her Lovers but she'd rather be hollow for she knows her very conception was an atrocity, a design assigned to keep captive those alienated from their True-Selves, she cries herself to sleep with feelings of inadequacy because she knows real men will never want her, a real man will never meet or know her embrace and the real men she helps to awaken who have fallen victim to her touch she knows will be gone soon, only a distant yet fond memory.

So, mother in less than 175 hours I will be releasing from prison, the first Historical Black College, the chrysalis, my surrogate mother, my Lover, my friend. And Yes, I am Happy, but I also am sad. I thought I'd never be institutionalized and here I am sitting with mixed emotions while contemplating leaving you. Even though I have had thoughts of lengthening my stay I must leave, there's a whole great wide world out there, my Dreams await, my fingerprint must be made and this time not in the county Justice Center but on the tables of history.

Mother, I know that you feel responsible because at the time of my birth you were a child yourself and a single parent unable to raise me, but the Truth is this has been better for me than worse. Look at the other 25 year olds with my background. =) Doesn't it make you smile and grateful when you see the progress and transformation I have made...? Whether she was my mother, Lover or friend she has held me, raised me, made me, REINVENTED ME AND CREATED SPACE FOR WHAT WAS ALWAYS THERE ALL

ALONG TO SHINE THROUGH! The time has come. It is finally my turn and I will take it. I WILL ACT NOW! And guess what… You don't have cancer silly you, you are alive and WELL, you're not dead. All your worries about dying before I was released can be put aside… YOU'RE HEALTHY! And you will witness my power, the same power that lies within you and EVERYONE ELSE! I Love you, I miss you and I cannot wait to see you!

Sincerely,

Your First Born

7= Divine Being – Goddess/God

Do you remember that ancient Delphic inscription above the forecourts of Apollo's Temple?

What did it say...? "KNOW THYSELF." KNOW THYSELF! This was not the first time that these words were made into commandment. They have been trumpeted amongst our species from the beginning of time from the Ancient Kemetic people to Jesus, Mohammed and now the New Age spiritualist and they will continue to be blasted into the ear of those who seek Truth and Understanding incessantly. These words, KNOW THYSELF are the answer to many questions that human beings have asked since day one. One of which is "Who is Goddess/God?"... The answer to that question, however, is another question... "Who Am I?" That is the question that has literally plagued us from caves to spaceships. Who am I? Who am I?? Who am I!? It has been enough to drive some to the far reaches of insanity and yet others to enlightenment. See I could tell you a million and one things ABOUT me, I could tell you that when I was four years old I was raped, that even before that it was decided my father wouldn't father ME, his one and only child. I could tell you that by the time I was 7 years old I had watched my mother's eye turn black more than any professional boxer I had ever seen. I could tell you that before I knew Algebra I knew how guns worked, that I held my aunty in my arms as she died overdosing on heroin. I could tell you about feeling afraid and internalizing my pain and anger because I was too scared to expose it. I could tell you about how I went from agnostic to evangelist and how I seemed to find drugs and sex to be one of the best coping skills that never Truly solved any of my problems on my journey of looking for a way out. I could tell you about being arrested for assaulting a woman I said I Loved or promoting prostitution of an innocent young woman. I am sure that DOC would Love it if I stopped there and that my criminal record, a piece of paper with some black ink stating that I had robbed, assaulted and stolen the dignity of another human being defined who I was for the rest of my Life but that is not who I am. These stories are only things that I have EXPERIENCED in my Life. They have been ACTIONS not ACTOR. THEY ARE NOT ME! They are not me? They are not me! But then I asked myself, WHO AM I? WHO AM I?? WHO AM I????

And then it came...

I am LIGHT!

I am LOVE!

I am Passion and Contentment!

I am Joy and I am Kindness!

I am Ambition and I am hope!

I am Empathy and I am Freedom.

I am Miraculous and-

I... AM... GOD!

I Am God!

I am a Divine aspect of the Infinite Consciousness! I am a Spirit in a body, NOT! to be confused with a body owning a spirit! My spirit is accompanying this body! It CHOSE this body to further its own development! It is not subject to the limitations of this physical realm which then means that I am not inescapably subject to the limitations of this socially constructed "reality"!

I am FREE!

In fact I never was captive except only in my OWN state of unconsciousness and YOU ARE FREE except in YOUR OWN state of unconsciousness!

It was after long suffering and pain that I had this realization. And I believe that it was made so by design. As I told you I was whitewashed by Colonial Christianity. For 21 years I was told to believe that Jesus was born a virgin and because of that I had to ask him for forgiveness and power to face another day. I don't know why this had never dawned on me sooner but even by Biblical account Jesus was brown, but Jesus "happened" to be white in colonial Christianity with blonde hair and blue eyes which meant I had to ask white men for forgiveness. I had to find my strength in white men and obey the every word of the white man. The same white man that owned and managed the entire system that was oppressing me so when I finally converted to Islam I thought that I had found some place of empowerment and that being a black man I had made a choice that would give me strength and internal fortitude. However, this too was not the height of my spirituality but rather a stepping stone to Al-Hawkk, The Ultimate Divine Truth. On my never ending path to seeking Truth and becoming more conscious, one religion poked holes in the former like a young prince finding fault in the old king he sought to overthrow eventually wearing out the pillars that held up the validity of the former ideology in my mind. Eventually, I grew tired of even the traditions of Islam. With all of the Wudhu and the Ghusl, the praying a mandatory minimum of 5 times a day and Salaam'ing everyone I came in contact with I just grew distant from the religion of it all (today I find a lot of the language, hadith and culture around Islam still to be BEAUTIFUL and I believe that the mannerism and characteristics of the prophet Muhammad (salallahu alahi wa salaam) and the real Jesus being practiced today would make any of us role model human beings almost 2000 years later).

Liberate the minds of human beings and ultimately you will liberate the bodies of them too.

-Marcus Garvey

I remember lying in bed inside my cell and reading a book that was punching holes in all sorts of fundamental beliefs I held. I was captivated by every page as I eagerly turned them. My spirit was resonating with ideas from cultures and dreams I myself had flirted with involving the powers of meditation, electromagnetism and altering what I perceived as the physical makeup of my body, objects, even reality. Some would call this "Mystical Magical Shit". However, in the stillness I had created with just becoming conscious of my breathing, reading and guarding my thoughts, I began to listen to that small voice in the back of my mind arguing against mainstream culture and inquiring if these were the natural states and fruits of human beings who had let go of the narratives society had passed down to us. Beings who had shifted their conscious thoughts to a place of abundance. Fruits of people who had begun to unlock one percent of their mind at a time reclaiming the gap between the 8% of our brain we use and the 100% we could be functioning from. As I read my mind was continuously opening up as if with every word I took in, a sinister cloud was being removed. I'm remembering the words "We are all aspects of the same infinite consciousness collectively we know as GOD" and feeling the warmth of the sun as a cloud outside rolled away and my cell lit up with light from its rays. It was my AHA! moment! It was the first time the idea of innate divinity transformed itself from a concept to an inherent embodiment of Universal Truth inside of my being. My body became warm and fuzzy and my energy peaked! With the biggest smile on my face I got up out of my bunk and ran to look in the mirror full of ecstatic Joy and Love radiating from my being. I looked in the mirror and repeated "YOU ARE GOD! YOU ARE LOVE!"… The two are inseparable.

The first step had been made into the spiritual from the intellectual. I had embodied the Universal Truth that we are all born with innate Divinity, Consciousness, Spirit and/or Love and that energy whatever you chose to name it was the thread that kept all of us, the ENTIRE UNIVERSE together with its creative and brilliant force. That collectively, the sum of ALL THINGS spirit is what I had known to call GOD. It was so liberating to believe that there was no cosmic judge passing on his evaluations of my Life. No being in the sky with a book and pen writing down or taking notes of my thoughts and deeds. No worries of a torturous afterlife with a snake tongued, spiked tail and pitchfork carrying little red demon waiting to burn my flesh eternally. Even more than those things the excitement and aliveness I was feeling with my vibrational frequency being set on LOVE was incredible! No one could do any wrong because I saw past the Maya, I saw past what they were presenting and saw into their spirit. I saw into them so deeply I could see them as a child and I could empathize and understand them there in those moments of full presence. Nothing was impossible to me in these moments of timeless time and space-less space. This was only the beginning. Re-membered with the consciousness of our eternal internal divinity and it was there all along. This whole time. I saw it in the Bible as I went back and read Jesus saying "I and the Father are one" John 10:30. Or I thought of the words the Prophet Muhammad had uttered "And We have already created man and know what his soul whispers to him, for We are closer to him than his jugular vein" in Surah Al-Qaf Ayat 16. It was what Buddhism and Hinduism had said for centuries, it was what Kemetic wisdom said ages before that! We do not need to look for god outside ourselves. Turning our focus internal and looking at what lies inside of us is how we find GOD!

"What lies behind us and what lies ahead of us are tiny matters compared to what lies within us."

Ralph Waldo Emerson

I AM THE EVIL ONE BUT I AM LOVE

I am the evil one

Fear (stone)

Anger (stick)

Emptiness (basket)

Grief (leaves)

Looking through my Life

See fear

See anger

See emptiness

See grief

Looking through my Life

Sitting with pain

Feeling all alone, nobody cares

But pain

Pain

But if pain then

Love

I AM Love

Love is still there

And She comforts me

Sometimes Love me or hate me attitudes

Distract

From the fact

That

Still you are Love-able

I AM LOVE

Eye dropped the idea of you and I and re-connected with the consciousness of interdependence. That WE are ALL ONE! Eye remembered that not too long ago we were all connected in LOVE, that we were not yet divided by the Maya in this Dunya and that we still saw each other as the Beloved. We had Agape for each other and in play and seriousness had spoken about our next upcoming adventure taking these bodies as vehicles to our destination of purification, education, fun and enlightenment. We had spoken about the tragic events we knew we would experience and the joyous occasions that would make it all worth Living. We Loved on one another because we knew that once embodying this human flesh we would only see the difference when we looked into each other's new face. We would judge and evaluate and forget that we are all siblings, friends and Lovers. It hurt our hearts to think that we could forget such an amazing and powerful Love, a Love that existed here in the dark, in the world vibrating at a frequency which was above what we would perceive once we took these bodies but with Love and desire for Truth we made our choice and we came into them. And Eye remember times when Eye saw you, or at least it seemed for a split second that Eye saw you in the mail-person, that Eye saw you in the person who came and cleaned up the dishes. Eye believe Eye saw you in the president, the judge even the police officer. Eye thought that I had seen you but my Mind told me that I had not... Until now. Now Eye see you and Eye remember you. Eye see you even when you do not see me. And although it hurts when you do not remember me Eye can remember the times when we were so in Love, the purest and best Love ever. The Love that was so sweet, so safe, and so warm, where Eye felt absolute joy in sharing my wild, creative and vulnerable self. Eye remember those times so when you pass me with no acknowledgement Eye smile. When you cross the street when you see me, Eye smile. When Eye reflect on the prison sentences that you blessed me with Eye smile still. Eye remember to smile when Eye reflect on when my earth mother screamed as your fist connected with her face or when you told me that you wanted a divorce. Eye smile because Eye remember our Love and Eye know that you will remember too. Even when you say you do not want to look for GOD Eye smile, because I know one day, even if by "accident", you will look INSIDE of YOURSELF and you will find GOD, and we will smile. We will smile together.

Eye heard it once said that it is Love that we must aim for. Any great archer knows that if there is any wind in the air they must compensate for that resistance and gravity as they train their arrow on the target. If they aim directly at the bullseye the resistance will force the arrow under the target as it decreases in velocity. This means even if ever so slightly it will still miss the intended target. When we pull back the bowstring of Social Change it is not enough to aim for Justice alone, no. With all the resistance that the forces we oppose provide if we aim for Justice, unfortunately it is inevitable we will fall short of even that. The great archer takes into consideration the opposing force when they aim their arrow and they aim above their target so that when the resistance comes it actually works in favor of the archer helping the arrow find its way on to the perfect path, the path the archer had intended it to take all along. Therefore like the great archer we must not aim for Social Justice we must aim for Love. In this way as we meet our resistance we smile because we remember our ultimate destination is a place between Love, Justice and Liberty for ALL of us.

I have decided to stick with love.
Hate is too great a burden to bear.
                    -Martin Luther King Jr.

As I sat there on my bed with ice cold rage pumping through my veins I realized the reason I was feeling angry, hurt and wanting with every fiber in my being to retaliate was because my needs for respect, connection, safety, harmony and fun were not being met. I had two options. I could be a "gangsta" (I.E. act from my animal, savage self) and get this man who I had allowed to offend me or I could allow evolution from Fight/Flight response into Social Engagement occur right here and now. I could act from my spiritual and intellectual self, utilizing self-empathy with some positive self-talk, affirmations and other coping skills I had learned throughout my years of incarceration. Maybe the most important skill, Visualization! See when I began to let go of the stereotypes, the traditions, the conditioning and all of the hype I could begin to see the King in me, begin to see the Pharaoh I was. I began to see the Ruler of MY Reality. I saw God in my beautiful Black body, I saw God in my beautiful Black mind, I saw God in my beautiful Black Spirit, in my soul I saw God and I saw The Creator of my Destiny. Having an inner-standing of who I TRULY am I had Inner Peace. Having inner Peace I was blessed to have even for a split second with all the hell breaking loose around and within me clarity of mind and with that clarity of mind I remembered my values and what I truly held dear to my heart. I remembered my goals, I remembered my strategies, the steps that would take me from point A to point Z and see all of my dreams and aspirations manifested and fulfilled! I saw the successful author, Life coach and CEO. I saw the happy father, I saw the man with knowledge of Self speaking with a gym full of young warriors in a juvenile detention center, redirecting their sharpened spears at the real and only true enemy of all mankind. Not only did I see, but I FELT. I felt the soft warm loving and nurturing embrace of my Earth. My Colombian Goddess, my Woman, the Wisdom to my Knowledge giving me all of the Understanding, Affection, Tranquility and Love that one man could need. I saw Life. In the midst of Death, I took a moment for observation and I saw Life! Sitting on my bunk with keys that opened the door to death I saw Life. Then I remembered as human beings every thought we dwell upon, every decision we make, every action we take is either out of Abundance or Scarcity, unmet need or needs met. Every decision is made out of Love or it is made out of Fear. You either allow Fear to cast its cloud around you fearing for your safety, your prosperity or what others may think of you or you STAND IN LOVE, embracing all that Life and the Universe has to offer you becoming a vessel for the Infinite Consciousness and the power of the cosmos to course through your being. You find yourself in tune with your inner divinity and when you tear down the walls of your conditioned Self and accept and embrace your inner divinity there is no need for a shank or any type of weapon because there is no place for violence… Why? Because the only battle to fight has already been won.

"Our deepest fear is not that we are inadequate. Our deepest fear is that we are powerful beyond measure. It is our light, not our darkness that most frightens us. We ask ourselves, who am I to be brilliant, gorgeous, talented, and fabulous? Actually, who are you not to be? You are a child of God. Your playing small does not serve the world. There is nothing enlightened about shrinking so that other people will not feel insecure around you. We are all meant to shine, as children do. We were born to make manifest the glory of God that is within us. It is not just in some of us; it is in everyone and as we let our own light shine, we unconsciously give others permission to do the same. As we are liberated from our own fear, our presence automatically liberates others."

-Marianne Williamson

This passage at times was the only thing that carried me safely to the next day. Times get hard, I get caught up in the Dunya, the Maya, society. I get pulled from the heights of my inner Peace into the depths of my Fear. We will all stray from the path we were privileged to see once awakened from our slumber, yet, if you were able to overcome the barriers placed upon your beautiful mind through the realization of yourself, Your TRUE Self, my Love, the Self consisting only of Peace, Love, Strength and Beauty, then believe me baby, YOU ASSUREDLY will find your way back to your path and continue to excel at being Amazing, achieving your wildest dreams and shining bright for the world to see as the shooting star you were born to be!

I Love YOU! I LOVE EACH AND EVERY ONE OF YOU!

"The revolution will FOREVER be in the hands of the young.
The young inherit the revolution."

-Huey P. Newton

P.E.A.C.E. From The Diamond G.A.N.G.

Zackery Max Driver

Co-Founder and visionary of Diamond G.A.N.G., creator of P.I.L.L.A.R.S. and Lover of Life. Driver's spirit and ambition will probably be the death of him. This beautiful being has found Liberation in the shackles and Light in the Darkness and is now passionately desiring to share what he has been privileged to learn with his community and the world at large.